THE 12

LAWS OF

SUCCESS

Habel .H. Samida

ISBN:1535054220
ISBN-13: 978-1535054225

DEDICATION

This book is dedicated to my family:
My soul met, Ann Assey and my amazing daughter,
Lightness.

CONTENTS

Author's Acknowledgments i

1 Forewords 1

2 Part One: You are the Success 3

3 Part Two: The 12 Laws for Success 8

4 Part Three: Your Decision, Your Destination 94

5 Part Four: About the Author 98

AUTHOR'S ACKNOWLEDGMENTS

Writing a book is a project that needs a lot of support from other people.

Thanks to Mike Ajao, Ken Stewart, Stanley Joseph, Raphael Chima, Antony Msangaa and Adam Nyando, for your assistance, encouragement and support in several areas of my life.

Finally, I'm forever grateful for YOU. Sure, you! The one reading this book. Thank you very much for taking your time to read this book. I really value your contribution. Without you I couldn't have been able to write this book. Therefore, I'm privileged and humbled to dedicate this book to you. As you open and read the pages, you will find out that you are very special to the universe and have the seed of greatness within you. And please, be reminded always

FOREWORDS

Congratulations on your exciting decision to read this book. You have made the right choice. I wrote this book because of dedicated people like you who wants to make a difference in life. I mean YOU. This is your course book with proven success laws which have transformed the lives of hundreds of thousands of people worldwide. So your life is going to be transformed as well by putting these principles into practice.

There are millions of self- development books published all over the world today, and yet, many more are published every single day. They are full of life transforming messages. But "THE TWELVE LAWS FOR SUCCESS" is a book you must read. It is unique and full of practical ways to transform your life in the way you never thought possible!

Your decision to read this book shows how much you are concerned in taking charge of your life. The author of this book believes that you have got the right tool and yet, the good news is you are going to discover few simple things that work like a miracle! But you have to be willing to use them, putting into practice day in day out, week in week out, soon you will start observing your life elevated to the new levels of happiness, wealth, abundance, health and prosperity.

This book gives you the twelve laws for achieving the success you desire. The laws written are the results of the findings from successful people in the world. As you open and read the pages, you will be able to learn from my own experience which comes from books I have ever read, tapes I listened to, seminars I attended and different successful people who have ever taught me.

The twelve laws for success are what makes some people successful and thriving while others unsuccessful and surviving. The understanding of these laws opens doors for you to kickstart your life.

In the second part, you will learn how *the inner your* controls *the outer you* in all aspects of your life. This inner part of you is your paradigm. It is what controls your life and mostly, holds you back from living your dream. However, it is the intention of this book to help you understand where your paradigm is coming from and how to start changing your paradigm through reading and repeating some affirmations given in the second part of the book. Changing your paradigm is the starting point of changing your life. This is non-negotiable.

Success is much easier, when you start thinking differently and change some of your behaviors which do not support success. This book guides you to get going and follow the steps in building successful habit. Remember, we are creatures of habit. As you discipline yourself to start transforming your habit, I can tell you; get ready to be surprised to discover the *great calumet copper mine* you have always walked on! Napoleon Hill the famous author of "think and grow rich" wrote in his books "the law of success in sixteen lessons;" *"Thousands of people walked over the great Calumet Copper Mine without discovering it. Just one lone man used his "imagination," dug down into the earth a few feet, investigated, and discovered the richest copper deposit on earth.*

You and every other person walk, at one time or another, over your "Calumet Mine." Discovery is a matter of investigation and use of "imagination." This book on the twelve Laws of Success *may lead the way to your "Calumet," and you may be surprised when you discover that you were standing right over this rich mine, in the work in which you are now engaged. In his lecture on "Acres of Diamonds," Russell Conwell tells us that we need not seek opportunity in the distance; that we may find it right where we stand!*

PART ONE

YOU are the success!

A human being can alter his life by altering his attitudes. ~William James

---

Meaning of SUCCESS in Life

What does SUCCESS means, exactly? It depends on who you ask. I'm serious! The only person that can prescribe the ultimate definition of success is you. Absolutely! Every person has different perspective about being prosperous in life and is defining success in another way, so there can't exist a definition that is suitable for all. It is very important that you know exactly how to define success in life! Make yourself aware what accomplishment, success and prosperity in general means to you in your life.

Some might define success as having millions of dollars, luxurious cars and a huge mansion, whereas others consider a life full of joy and happiness with their family as the true meaning of success. Once you have figured out what is important for you personally you are able to focus on your visions and goals.

However, I consider the general meaning of success as living your life in a way that pleases you or getting whatever you desire and becoming the kind of a person you always wanted to be.

Success begins with your attitude and how you take the steps necessary in the right direction. It is the process that takes commitment in molding your habit and discipline yourself in following them consistently until you plant them to your subconscious mind. Start learning to maintain a positive focus in life no matter what is going on around you. Stay focused on successes rather than obstacles and your past failures. Look only in the positive side of life and be committed to discipline yourself to keep on keeping on. The more you follow the right steps in the right direction, the more you handle all the distractions and fulfill your goals.

You create much of your own happiness, wealth, health and abundance with how you respond to your situation and how you approach life. When you develop the habit of having definite major goals and always thinking about all the possibilities, open doors, opportunities and focusing only on the goodness of things in life and seeing the best, life goes so much better than you can ever begin to imagine. That's how you have success in life despite what's happening around you.

How you behave determines what kind of life you're going to have. When you behave like a successful person, you must become one. If you don't follow, there is no way you are going to succeed! You can find this out by simply looking at your life right now. Ask yourself; how does it look like? The answer to that is the reflection of how you behave towards success. Let me say it straight. If you are not successful, you simply don't follow successful principles. Your behavior controls your activities, and activities give the results called *your life*.

Your behaviors come from your belief system, and your belief system comes from your attitude of mind. Listen to me! We mostly behave from what we believe. Therefore, if you want to change your behavior, change what causes your attitude; that is your *success chart*. Your success chart is the way you believe towards success. It is resulted by how you have been programmed by your environment through learning about success since when you were very young. This book will help you understand different ways of learning that resulted to your programming. You will also learn how to reprogram your mind for success.

It is possible for you to be successful because, inside of you there's a person you don't know. There's a seed of greatness. If you can figure this out, you are unstoppable! Successful entrepreneurs, athletes, musicians, authors, leaders, and all successful people in all walks of life were able to make it when they changed their inner games in the first place, believed in themselves and then get fired up or became *hungry* as Les Brown used to say.

YOUR DREAMS ARE POSSIBLE! Believe in yourself. Sadly, too many of us are not stretching to reach them simply because we pay attention to other people who tell us our dreams are foolish, or we can't reach them. There's an old, well known story of a chicken farmer who found an eagle's egg. He put it with his chickens and soon the egg hatched.

The young eagle grew up with all the other chickens and whatever they did, the eagle did too. He thought he was a chicken, just like them.

Since the chickens could only fly for a short distance, the eagle also learnt to fly a short distance. He thought that was what he was supposed to do. So that was all that he thought he could do. As a consequence, that was all he was able to do.

One day the eagle saw a bird flying high above him. He was very impressed. "Who is that?" he asked the hens around him. "That's the eagle, the king of the birds," the hens told him. "He belongs to the sky. We belong to the earth, we are just chickens." So the eagle lived and died as a chicken, for that's what he thought he was.

I want to encourage you today that you are an eagle. You may have been brought up in a situation that limited your understanding of your potential, but it's time now for the past to lose its hold on you. Don't die thinking you're a chicken. Soar high, just as you were meant to. Be all that you are meant to be!

You are able to accomplish anything you want. Believe me, you can make it, don't seek for approval from other people. Know in your heart that you have the seed of greatness within and remind yourself every single day as you look yourself in the mirror. Reminding yourself everyday will not only refrain you from looking for other people's approval but also wanting to have people like, accept and be nice to you. Because the bad news is, you cannot make people approve, like, love, understand, validate, accept or be nice to you. You can't control them either. Good news is, it doesn't matter. It doesn't matter what other people think or say, do not care! They don't change the fact that you have the seed of greatness within you. Mind your own business. Be reminded that, your business is to make a difference. Stay on track.

This book is also going to open your mind to accomplish more than what you have accomplished right now in case you are in your comfort zone. It ignites the feeling of being *uncomfortable*, that will make you stretch for the new levels. You deserve more regardless how big your achievement is! You have to set for new bigger goals to achieve. Be uncomfortable. I don't mean you become ungrateful. I mean, *stretch yourself to accomplishing another dream which is much bigger than the previously one.* Don't settle where you are right now, you are not destined there. You are MORE!

Its inspiring reading the words by Jean Houston. YOU ARE MORE.

You are more than you pretend to be
You are more than what most eyes can see
You are more than all your history
Look inside and you will find
There's glory in your mind
Come be the kind of person you would be....
You are more than what your leaders say
You are more than how you earn your pay
You are more than what you seem today
So drop that loser's mask
You're equal to the task
The question you should ask is who you are....
You are more than what the preachers shout
You are more, come let your spirit out
You are more, your soul shall have no doubt
Arise, become awake
With every breath you take
The god within will ache to be....
You are more than some statistic chart
You are more than the sum of all your parts
You are more inside your heart of hearts
You know that it is true
This being that is you
Has miracles to do
Believe....

Don't feel comfortable, you have to set higher goals to accomplish. Your business is not over yet! Greatness is waiting in the other side of your comfort zone. You are capable of achieving more than what you have. Moreover, you will not understand how much you can accomplish in your lifetime. Human being has never used more than fifteen percent of his ability, no matter how many big things he has accomplished in his life. Unfortunately, most of us do not use even five percent of our abilities! Don't die with your music in you. Sing like no one is listening. Dance like no one is seeing you and love like you have no any idea of being hurt. You deserve the best life has to offer. Claim!

PART TWO

The 12 Laws for Success

Law #1
Prepare the inner YOU.

Your inner world creates your outer world. ~ T. Harv Eker

The facts show that ninety nine percent of people have been programmed to let their outside world control the inside! This is against the law of success. For you to be successfully financially, or other major areas of your life, you must let your inner world control the outer. This is the reason why many people are not living their dreams.

Before hitting your financial breakthrough in the physical world, you have to experience it in your mind. It may sound strange to you, but it is exactly that. Anything appearing in the outer world started in the inner world. I mean, your thoughts are the cause of your behaviors, your behaviors overtime results to your habit. And the habit overtime creates the circumstances called "your life"

Your thoughts however are controlled by your paradigm. Your paradigm is the way your mind has been conditioned or programmed to think. And that is what controls your life. I think you want to know how the programming takes place.

Well, here is how.

When you were young, you probably heard, saw and experienced things about wealth, rich and success generally. These ideas and information were stored in form of files to your subconscious mind. And the truth is; these files run your life. They make a set of your character, beliefs and integrity. Anything new that comes inform of thought and idea can be processed and then translated through your attitude built from these files.

You cannot act beyond what you believe and the way you have been programmed. That's why you cannot get different results by doing things with the same mental attitude. The first step you have to take in changing your life is to reprogram your mind. Replace all the files with the one that supports your journey for success.

This chapter will show you how to reprogram your mind by placing the right files through reading and repeating some affirmations on money, wealth, prosperity and abundance

By changing your thinking you will be in the fast track to change your life. Your thoughts create your reality. Practice positive thinking. Act the way you want to be, and soon you will be the way you act. Dedicate yourself to renewing your mind, so that you can begin to live free of doubt, fear and negative thoughts. Master your mind or your mind will master you!

Let your inner game run the outer! Not the opposite. You become who you are outside by who you are inside. No matter where you reach in the outer world, if you haven't built your inner self to deserve it, your unconscious mind will direct you to do the things that will take you back to where you belong in your inner world. In other words, if you have poverty conscious in your subconscious mind, you are likely to lose everything you get because your subconscious mind will remind you of what you think and believe. Sooner or later you are going to be exactly what you really think you are! Statistics shows that, most of the people who get rich by winning lottery end up just broke as they were in a short period of time. Do you know the reason? I'll tell you. It's because, deep inside their subconscious mind they still feel poor. So their mind will prove it right. It will not deviate from its self image.

I have heard of many successful people who teach this principle by giving out their own examples of losing everything, when they just got rich in the physical world but inside they still had poor mentality. It was when they managed to build their inside world, when they experienced true success.

The lack of money is not a problem. It's just a sign or an indicator to show what is taking place in your mind! For that being the case, you have something to do. Make it your business to stay positive and focused on what you see as the best possible outcome for your life. Do the inner work that will help you to build and maintain a positive attitude, a stronger faith, and courage for the road ahead. Remember that you don't need any miracle power because you already have. What you really need is for you to discover them. You're the next success story to be told.

What you think most of the time is what you become. If you desire to get rich and achieve financial goals, starts now thinking and acting like a millionaire. If you want to be health, or lose some pounds, feel yourself the way you want to be. Imagine the excitement you are going to have and how that cloth is going to fit you. If you desire to be an athlete, musician, author, pursue a degree or anything, imagine yourself walking on that stage, singing in front of hundreds of thousands, appearing in the list of bestselling authors and so on. There is a miraculous power in imagination. It is the only way that will condition your mind to think of what you want in life and to work for it without even thinking of it since it will become your nature. Therefore it will always remind yourself doing what it takes to achieve your life goals.

Begin to think success if you want to succeed. Accomplishment starts in the mind, that's why Napoleon Hill wrote the book "think and grow rich". Thinking works like a magnet to attract whatever you want. Make your business to mold your thinking so you become who you think you are. It has bees said "as a man think so he shall become" it doesn't say as the man does so shall become! What is the difference? The way you think affects your activities. And these activities lead to results. Therefore, in changing the results, you have to change what? Your thoughts, you got it! Changing your life starts with changing the way you think. Negative thought will keep holding you back. It is what we call poverty consciousness that digs deep inside the unconscious level which makes you believe you are not worthy to have more money and access for financial breakthrough.

When it comes to accessing financial breakthrough, it would be incredible if you do things differently. I mean, you have to think the way rich people think. Rich people think differently from poor and the mediocre. I hope you asked yourself "how do rich people think?" well, this book is going to give you the guidance so that you can start thinking exactly the same as rich people. This will not only transform your paradigm, but also your financial status and lifestyle.

We are living in the universe where there are laws operating to everyone, at any time. They don't care whether you know them or not. They are just there and influencing our lives. One of the laws that are very crucial in building our inner world to attract success is the *Law of Attraction*. This can be understood by understanding the "coincidence" or "like attracts like". What this means is that, we are responsible for bringing any influence in our lives, whether positive or negative. This happens without caring whether we realize it or not!

Let me give you an example that will help you understand this clearly. Have you ever thought of calling someone, when you touch your phone you realize the phone ringing, when you pick up you realize it's the one calling? Or have you ever thought of getting a particular car and certainly you see that kind of car everywhere? The key part of understanding how this law works is to place your focus on how it can have an intense impact on what happens to you.

If you spend your valuable time thinking on how you cannot reach your financial breakthrough, the past experience, fears of the future, you name it. You're likely to see exactly the same stuff appearing in your life. But if you look for the silver lining in every experience you'll soon start to see possibilities, abundance and opportunities surrounding you. However, the Law of attraction opens your eyes to see the freedom you have in taking control of your life by shaping it in the direction you want.

Learning how this law works also helps you in monitoring your thoughts by getting rid of any toxic ideas or thoughts that doesn't empower your dreams. You will be able to encourage powerful thoughts which are leading to your destination. In other words I can say, becoming more mindful of your own thoughts helps you to see even discover what you should keep or remove from your own mind and the reality you experience. The reason is that, you will become more sensitive in underlying negativity and starting to replace it with new beliefs and feelings that better reflect positive vision of your future. This ongoing focus on self-reflection elevates your focus on what you really want for your future, and you can then progress to setting some clearer strategies for your action plan.

Learn to incorporate your understanding of the law of attraction into your daily life by letting it shape you. Practice it from morning to night, day in day out, week in week out, month in month out. At the beginning it might sound like an overwhelming undertaking, but the truth is that; these are simple but powerful changes with astonishing results! Embrace it and I promise you, it will not only become second nature, but also literally change your life.

How to reprogram your mind

Let go all the limited ideas about success. Take time; turn your television off and anything that will distract you. You can either go to a place where you will have nothing to distract your mind. Have a pen and a notebook with you. Start by writing all the statements or phrases you have ever heard about success in every key area of your life and think on how they have been limiting your success. Here are some of the phrases about money by T. Harv Eker in his book "The Secret of the Millionaire Mind". *Money is the root of all evil, save your money for a rainy day, rich people are greedy, rich people are criminals, filthy rich, you have to work hard to make money, money doesn't grow on trees, you can't be rich and spiritual, money doesn't buy happiness, money talks, the rich get richer and the poor get poorer, that's not for people like us, not everyone can be rich, there's never enough, we can't afford it.* You name it!

Start feeding your mind with powerful money, wealth, prosperity and abundance affirmations. At this stage, you are now on your way to start reprogramming your subconscious mind by feeding it with positive messages about money, wealth, prosperity and abundance. You need to have the message repeated over and over again, everyday. This will make your mind start thinking about success in a positive way.

You can create affirmations about the kind of accomplishment you want. For example; if you want to buy a home, you can create an affirmation like "I live in a beautiful home". Create an affirmation in present tense and start feeling and imagining yourself living in that home. Do it for anything you desire. Furthermore, I am giving you some affirmations for you to be reading and repeating them over and over again. These affirmations are divided into four; *money, wealth, prosperity* and *abundance*. Each of those has several sets of affirmations. You may like to start with one section at a time. Also feel free to choose affirmations you like the best, combine them and repeat them regularly to attract the blessings in the form of money, wealth, prosperity and abundance into your life.

Be committed to practice this strategy, because it is the proven method of reprogramming your mind to start thinking in a positive way. Do it for your own life. I believe that you create much of your own happiness, wealth, health and abundance with how you reprogram your mind to think about success, something that will change the way you approach life. When you develop the new habit of thinking positively about success, your mind will shift to the new paradigm of "success conscious" and it will always direct you into thinking of all the possibilities, open doors, opportunities and focusing only on the goodness of things in life and seeing the best. It is the point where life goes so much better than you can ever begin to imagine. That's how you have success in life despite what's happening around you.

The following are the affirmations. They are divided into four; *money, wealth, prosperity* and *abundance*. Each of those has several sets of affirmations for you to be reading and repeating them over and over again. You may like to start with one section at a time, but feel free to choose affirmations you like the best, combine them and repeat them regularly to attract the blessings in the form of money, wealth, prosperity and abundance into your life.

A. MONEY AFFIRMATIONS
Set #1

1. I feel Rich

2. I love money. Money loves me.

3. I attract money now

4. I am very happy and grateful that money comes to me in increasing quantities from many sources on a continuous basis

5. I am receiving money now

6. I have more than enough money

7. I am willing, ready and able to receive money

8. I see abundance everywhere

9. I am a money magnet

10. I am grateful for what I already have and for all that I receive now.

11. I have more than what I need

12. Money now comes to me from unexpected sources and I am grateful

13. My income is growing higher and higher

14. I am a rich child of a loving universe

15. I have the power to attract money

16. I receive money happily now

17. Money flows to me easily

18. I am sensible with money and manage it wisely.

19. I allow my income to constantly expand and I always live in comfort and joy

Set #2

1. I realize that money is essential for leading a good life but that I should not make it the number one priority of life.

2. The Universe is the constant supplier of money for me and I always have enough money to fulfill my needs.

3. Whatever activities I perform make money for me and I am always full of money.

4. My bank balance is increasing everyday and I always have enough money for myself.

5. Money and I are friends and our friendship will never fall apart.

6. I am a money magnet towards whom money is constantly attracted.

7. Every day I am attracting and saving more and more money.

8. Money is an integral part of my life and is never away from me.

9. I am debt free as money is constantly flowing into my life.

10. My money consciousness is always increasing and keeping me surrounded by money.

11. I have a positive money mindset

12. I am focused on becoming rich

13. Attracting money is easy

14. My bank account worth is always growing

15. Money is good, money is energy, money is power

16. I am fully supported making money doing what I love to do.

17. Money comes to me through both expected and unexpected channels

18. My income automatically rises higher and higher

Set #3

1. I am open to best things in life

2. My wallet is overflowing with money

3. Life is so easy

4. I welcome money into my life.

5. I am open and ready to let money into my life.

6. The money is in my life just as natural as eating, drinking and sleeping.

7. Money simply falls into my lap

8. My pockets are full of money

9. My positive money thoughts are coming true

10. The universe always serves my highest interest

11. I can always get whatever I need

12. Financial success is mine, I accept it now

13. I love having money

14. There is enough for everyone

15. I attract money naturally

16. My middle name is money.

17. The more I contribute for others, the more money I make

18. The more I enjoy life, the more money I make

Set #4

1. The Universe constantly supplies money to me.

2. I always have enough money to fulfill my needs.

3. Money and I are friends.

4. Money is flowing to me.

5. Money flows easily into my life.

6. I attract money to me and I am attracted to money.

7. I love money.

8. I enjoy making money and strive to have fun in every aspect of my work.

9. Whatever activities I perform make money for me.

10. Money flows to me easily, frequently, and abundantly.

11. I have the power to attract money.

12. I place no limits on the amount of money I can make.

13. I attract money naturally.

14. My bank account is filled with money.

15. I have an endless supply of cash.

16. I attract money everywhere I go.

17. I do have a source of financial flow.

18. Today is the day of my amazing good fortune.

Set #5

1. I happily see every bill paid now.

2. I joyfully see every obligation met now.

3. I am boundless abundance in radiant expression.

4. I am bountifully supplied with money.

5. I accept all the joy and prosperity life has to offer.

6. Financial success comes to me easily and effortlessly.

7. My income exceeds my expenses.

8. My grateful heart is a magnet that attracts more of everything I desire.

9. I am a money magnet and prosperity of all kinds is drawn to me.

10. Today is a delightful day. Money comes to me in expected and unexpected ways.

11. I spend money under direct inspiration wisely and fearlessly, knowing my supply is endless and immediate.

12. An avalanche of money is coming my way.

13. I am happily enjoying a lifestyle of luxury.

14. I now live in a rich and loving universe.

15. This is a rich universe and there is plenty for all of us.

Set #6

1. I am now accumulating large sums of Money.

2. Money flows in my life.

3. I always have more Money coming in than going out.

4. I am increasingly magnetic to Money.

5. I create Money through joy, aliveness, and self-love.

6. As I do what I love, Money flows freely to me.

7. Money comes to me easily and effortlessly.

8. My savings act as a magnet to draw more Money.

9. All the Money I spend enriches society and comes back to me multiplied.

10. All the Money I spend and earn brings me joy.

11. All my Money is energy awaiting my command to create good in my life.

12. All my Money is working for me to increase my abundance, joy and aliveness.

13. My Money is a source of good for myself and others.

14. I feel good about all the Money I spend.

15. Money flows freely and abundantly into my life.

16. A constant flow of Money is coming to me from Known and Unknown Sources!

17. I feel good about Money and deserve it in my life.

18. I am thankful for the comfort and joy that Money provides me.

Set #7

1. I release all my negative beliefs about Money and invite wealth into my life.

2. Making Money is good for me and for everyone in my life.

3. My Money is growing higher and higher now.

4. Money is an important part of my life and is never away from me.

5. I clearly see opportunities to effortlessly make Money.

6. Money always flows to me easily.

7. I am magnetic to Money, and it is magnetic to me.

8. Money flows freely in my life.

9. All the money I need is flowing to me

10. All of the money I could ever want is flowing to me now.

11. I always have enough money

12. I have all of the money, time, talent and energy to accomplish all that I desire.

13. Money is coming to me every day.

14. Money now comes to me in abundance in perfect ways

15. The more money I have, the more money I can use to help myself and others

16. The more money I have the more money I have to give

17. Money is always circulating freely in my life and there is always a surplus

18. Money flows to me like a waterfall

B. WEALTH AFFIRMATIONS.
    <u>Set #1</u>

1. I welcome all the things money can buy

2. All my bills are paid with wonderful ease

3. I am passionate about building wealth

4. I give thanks that I am now rich, wealthy and happy

5. I have the power to attract wealth

6. I receive money and wealth in unique ways

7. All resistance in me to receive more wealth has dissolved in total grace

8. Wealth and Money comes to me easily & effortlessly

9. I create money, wealth, joy and happiness in my life

10. I am increasingly magnetic towards money and wealth

11. All the money I need is already waiting to reach me

12. I let go of all my fears about money

13. I let go of all my inhibitions about money

14. I spend money without fear

15. There is plenty of wealth in my life

16. Money is an energy and it flows freely through me now

17. All my blockages to receive money have now dissolved

18. Everything I need to generate wealth is available to me right now

Set #2

1. I am wealthy right now

2. I am worthy of receiving more wealth

3. I love myself, as a wealthy person

4. I am an abundantly wealthy person

5. Wealth flows to me

6. My positive affirmations bring me wealth and prosperity

7. My self-worth and net worth are increasing

8. Wealth floats around me continuously

9. I am passionate about building wealth

10. I give thanks that I am now rich, wealthy and happy

11. I have the power to attract wealth

12. I receive money and wealth in unique ways

13. There is plenty of wealth in my life

14. All resistance in me to receive more wealth has dissolved in total grace

15. Wealth comes to me easily and effortlessly

16. My mind is open to the infinite supply of wealth

17. I allow wealth to follow freely and generously in my life

18. I attract ideal circumstances and opportunities to increase my net worth

Set #3

1. I accept and embrace wealth in my life.

2. I am skilled at creating assets that make me wealthy.

3. I respect my abilities to generate wealth.

4. I am living the life of my wealthy dreams.

5. The Universe has chosen me to be wealthy so that I can help others with my wealth.

6. I believe anyone can be wealthy — and that includes me.

7. I recognize and embrace wealth building opportunities.

8. Every day is a wealthy day.

9. If others can be wealthy, so can I.

10. I am always immersed in wealth.

11. I am passionate about building wealth

12. I see myself as wealthy and that's who I am

13. Wealth is my birthright, and I claim wealth for myself now.

14. Through my power of intention, I effortlessly attract all the wealth I desire and need.

15. Great Wealth is flowing to me NOW.

16. I create Wealth easily and effortlessly.

17. I dissolve all false messages around creating Wealth.

Set #4

1. I have a Wealth of valuable skills and talents.

2. My wealth situation improves every second of every day.

3. I see myself as wealthy, and that's who I am.

4. I choose wealth and abundance.

5. My wealth derives from honesty in everything I do.

6. Wealth is my birth-right, my natural state of being.

7. All my issues with wealth have disappeared.

8. I am wealthy.

9. Whatever I do, it always ends in amassing wealth.

10. Every day in every way, my wealth is increasing.

11. I am gracious for the wealth I have in my life.

12. Being wealthy gives me joy, happiness and peace of mind.

13. I realize that I can help others with my wealth; so I stay wealthy.

14. I allow my passions to perpetuate good in the world through my wealth.

15. Wealth is a positive expression of divine energy.

16. I release all negativity around building wealth.

17. I release all opposition to wealth.

18. I have the wealth to be successful.

C. PROSPERITY AFFIRMATIONS
   Set #1.

1. I am prosperous, wealthy and happy.

2. I am easily attracting all the wealth that I desire into my life.

3. Prosperity and abundance comes to me easily and effortlessly

4. It is easy for me to become prosperous.

5. I am worthy to have abundance and prosperity.

6. I am a magnet to prosperity and abundance.

7. All the wealth I have brings me joy.

8. I will always have more than enough wealth and prosperity.

9. I am attracting financial prosperity

10. I am and will always be prosperous

11. I deserve to prosper.

12. I know that the world is prosperous.

13. It is so easy for me to open to prosperity.

14. My net worth is always increasing

15. My wealth is increasing regularly making prosperous.

16. The whole universe is conspiring to make me prosperous

17. I am thankful for the prosperity in my life

Set #2

1. I am prosperous

2. Prosperity is my birthright

3. My life is prosperous

4. Prosperity is mine.

5. I give generously to myself and others

6. I see prosperity everywhere

7. I attract prosperity like a powerful magnet.

8. I give thanks for the prosperity which is mine.

9. Wealth and prosperity is circulating in my life.

10. My circumstances are changing and prosperity is flowing into my life.

11. I create prosperity in my life.

12. I notice prosperity all around me.

13. Prosperity is mine and I choose to live it.

14. I create prosperity easily and effortlessly

15. Prosperity is within me, prosperity is around me

16. I enjoy my prosperity and share it freely with the world

17. All resistance to prosperity has dissolved in total grace

18. My prosperity is unlimited, my success is unlimited now

Set #3

1. I was prosperous, I'm prosperous and will always be prosperous.

2. I always have whatever I need. The Universe takes good care of me.

3. My life is full of love and joy and all the material things that I need.

4. Prosperity within me, prosperity around me

5. I allow all good things to come into my life and I enjoy them.

6. I let go of all resistance to prosperity and it comes to me naturally.

7. Prosperity surrounds me, prosperity fills me and prosperity flows to me and through me.

8. I am a magnet for money. Prosperity of every kind is drawn to me.

9. I move from poverty thinking to prosperity thinking and my finances reflect this change.

10. I now draw from the abundance of the spheres my immediate and endless supply. All Channels are free! All Doors are open!

11. I now release the gold-mine within me. I am linked with an endless golden stream of prosperity which comes to me under grace in perfect ways.

12. Prosperity of all kinds are drawn to me Now!

13. Compliments are Gifts of Prosperity and I accept them graciously!

14. Every day I grow more financially prosperous!

15. I love prosperity and I attract it naturally.

16. The whole Universe and entire mankind is conspiring to make me prosperous and abundant.

17. I deserve all good in my life and that includes prosperity

18. My income is constantly increasing and I prosper wherever I turn!

Set #4

1. I believe I have the right to be prosperous and successful.

2. I am abundant, healthy, happy and live in prosperous

3. I deserve to prosper in everything I do.

4. It is so easy to open to prosperity.

5. I can be prosperous.

6. I was prosperous, am prosperous and will always be prosperous.

7. Every day in every way I am becoming more and more prosperous

8. Everything and ever body prospers me now

9. I now draw the highest, best, and most prosperous minded people to me

10. All resistance to prosperity dissolves away.

11. Prosperity flows to me at all times, in all ways.

12. I allow prosperity.

13. Every day I am growing more financially prosperous.

14. I prosper wherever I turn and I know that I deserve prosperity of all kinds

15. I am happy, healthy and prosperous.

16. I exude passion, purpose and prosperity.

17. I send others thoughts of their increased prosperity.

18. My prosperity prospers others.

Set #5

1. I trust the universal spirit of prosperity to provide richly for me now.

2. I accept prosperity and Abundance into my life.

3. My beliefs create my reality. I believe in my unlimited prosperity.

4. My prosperity thoughts create my prosperous world.

5. I speak of success and prosperity. My words uplift and inspire others.

6. I recognize my true Source and let prosperity pour forth into my every experience.

7. I give thanks that the prosperity which is mine by Divine Right, NOW pours in and piles up under grace in perfect ways.

8. My prosperity is unlimited. My success is unlimited NOW.

9. Everything and everybody prospers me NOW and I prosper everything and everybody NOW.

10. I love the highest and best in all people and I NOW draw the highest, best, and most prosperous minded people to me.

11. The prospering truth now sets me free.

12. I am destined to find Prosperity in everything I do.

13. I know there is ample Prosperity for all.

14. Prosperity now happens to me.

15. I let go of all resistance to Prosperity, and it comes to me naturally.

16. I am worthy of receiving Prosperity now.

17. Prosperity and abundance surround me.

18. I attract Prosperity with each thought I think.

Set #6

1. I have everything I need right now to accomplish everything I want.

2. The riches of the universe come to me effortlessly.

3. I am a lucky, happy, healthy and successful person

4. The possibilities of the universe are flowing to me

5. I live a charmed life

6. I am safe, all my needs are met

7. I already have everything I need

8. I have everything I need to get everything I want

9. I deserve the good life

10. I deserve to be happy

11. I give generously, and receive graciously

12. My prosperity contributes to the prosperity of others

13. I am eager to give more than I am paid for

14. I respect my abilities and always work to my full potential.

15. I am a positive resource and people want to do business with me

16. Golden living, loving well-being is mine.

17. All my properties are cash-flow positive

18. I will be productive and prosperous today.

19. I am prosperous in everything I do

D. ABBUNDANCE AFFIRMATIONS.
   Set #1

1. Abundance is mine.

2. I am living an abundantly happy life.

3. I can see abundance everywhere around me.

4. I absolutely attract abundance.

5. I believe that more abundance is coming to me now.

6. Abundance is within me, abundance is around me.

7. The Universe wants me to have great abundance.

8. I am easily led to the abundance, I desire.

9. I am deserving of abundance, no matter what.

10. I allow the universe to bless me with great abundance now.

11. My good now flows to me in streams of success, happiness and abundance.

12. I am so grateful now that I possess abundance.

13. I deserve to have financial abundance in my life now.

14. Abundance and I are one.

15. I enjoy an abundance of money.

16. I have unlimited abundance.

17. I expect lavish abundance every day in every way.

18. All I have to do is ask for abundance and allow it.

Set #2

1. I am living abundantly

2. Abundance flows easily when I relax

3. Feeling joyful attracts abundance

4. I love abundance in all its beautiful forms

5. I am relaxing into greater abundance

6. Abundance is my divine birthright

7. I always have more than enough abundance

8. Thank you universe for my great abundance

9. The more abundantly I live the more abundance I will receive.

10. I open to the flow of abundance in all areas of my life.

11. I can easily imagine myself having limitless abundance

12. My grateful heart draws abundance like a magnet

13. This day is filled with endless expressions of abundance

14. My consistent focus on abundance draws it to me

15. I love the idea of having truly effortless abundance

16. Abundance around me, abundance within me, abundance throughout me.

17. Today I expand my awareness of the abundance around me

18. I live in an abundant world. All is perfect in my universe.

Set #3

1. Perfect abundance is my chosen reality

2. Abundance flows to me

3. Abundance is my birth right

4. The whole universe is conspiring to make me abundant

5. I am thankful for the abundance in my life

6. I am prosperous, healthy, happy and live in abundance

7. I love abundance and I attract it naturally

8. I believe I have the right to be Abundant, and successful.

9. I am abundant

10. I will live life abundantly

11. I am willing to be more abundant now

12. I will live the abundant life

13. All my needs are met instantaneously

14. My life is full of love and joy, and all the material things that I need

15. My mind is a powerful magnet for riches and abundance

16. My supply is endless, inexhaustible and immediate

17. I am thankful for the unlimited flow of good into my life.

18. I now release the goldmine within me

Set #4

1. I know that life is abundant and I accept abundance in my life now

2. I open to the flow of great abundance in all areas of my life.

3. I love life and accept my abundance unconditionally

4. I am Unlimited! I am Abundant! I am Worthy and Deserving of all Good!

5. Creative Energy flows through All areas of my Life and Abundantly!

6. Cash moves in abundant amounts in my Life!

7. I am in a state of fulfillment, have abundant love and joy in my life and am free to do whatever I wish to do.

8. My business is an all consuming love affair and I attract whatever I need through it.

9. I always have more than enough of everything I need.

10. My income is constantly increasing

11. My good comes from everywhere and everyone

12. New opportunities to increase my income open up for me now

13. I allow the universe to bless me in surprising and joyful ways.

14. My grateful heart is a magnet that attracts more of everything I desire.

15. My day is filled with limitless potential in joy, abundance and love.

16. I am overflowing with Abundant Prosperity!

17. Abundance is my birthright and I have it.

18. Abundance within me, abundance around me.

Set #5

1. I allow abundance.

2. I now realize my plan for abundant living.

3. The more grateful I am, the more reasons I find to be grateful

4. I pay my bills with love as I know abundance flows freely through me.

5. There is abundance in the universe for every living being.

6. Today I expand my awareness of the abundance all around me.

7. I feel the love, the joy, the abundance.

8. I am wide awake to my abundance

9. I serve only faith and my unlimited Abundance is made manifest.

10. Life is easy; I have an Abundance of whatever I need.

11. Abundance surrounds me. Today I claim my share.

12. I am now on the royal road of Success, Happiness and Abundance, all the traffic goes my way.

13. My good NOW flows to me in a steady, unbroken, ever-increasing stream of success, happiness and Abundance.

14. I was destined to be prosperous. I have Abundance to share and to spare.

15. I fill my mind with the idea of Abundance, and Abundance manifests in all my affairs.

16. The presence of joy in my heart releases an Abundance of good in my life.

17. I expect lavish Abundance every day in every way in my life and affairs.

18. I welcome and enthusiastically accept unlimited Abundance.

Set #6

1. My financial Abundance overflows today.

2. Abundance is limited only by my unconsciousness.

3. My life is filled with an Abundance of good.

4. With Source to guide me, my life is filled with joyous successes and rich Abundance.

5. I release all feelings of lack and limitation and joyfully accept blessings of joy and Abundance.

6. Abundance is mine! I give thanks for the unlimited flow of good into my life.

7. Gratitude moves me from perceptions of lack to manifestations of Abundance in all facets of my life.

8. I am the source of my Abundance.

9. I picture Abundance for myself and others.

10. I deserve Abundance.

11. I trust my ever-increasing ability to create Abundance.

12. I am linked with the unlimited Abundance of the universe.

13. I have Abundance in every area of my life.

14. I bless the Abundance I see in others.

15. The universe is safe, abundant and friendly.

16. I live in an abundant universe. I always have everything I need.

17. I am abundantly provided for as I follow my path.

18. I choose to live an abundant life.

Set #7

1. My greatest good is coming to me now.

2. Today is filled with opportunity, and I will seize it.

3. Everything good is coming to me easily and effortlessly.

4. I can and will have more than I ever dreamed possible.

5. Like a powerful magnet, I attract all my desires in great abundance.

6. I am certain that my path is always perfect for me.

7. I am extremely successful.

8. I deserve the best and it comes to me now.

9. My possibilities are endless.

10. I have everything I need, to achieve every goal I have.

11. My work is deeply satisfying.

12. At every step, good opportunity appears before me.

13. I easily, openly and freely accept abundance, every moment!

14. I am thankful for the infinite, abundant source of my abundance.

15. I see right through hindrances and obstructions and know that abundance is all mine.

16. I am a grateful person receiving the abundant blessings of the loving Universe.

17. I have creativity and energy in abundance

18. The Universe fulfills my every desire

Set #8

1. I possess an abundant supply of creativity.

2. Giving reaffirms the abundance mentality

3. I am enthusiastic about all of my projects

4. I have unlimited potential. Only good lies before me.

5. I am open and receptive to all the good and abundance in the universe. Thank you creator.

6. My life flows effortlessly as doors of opportunity open to me everywhere in every aspect of my life.

7. I always find an abundance of things to love about my life, myself, and all those around me.

8. I am creating an abundance of clients in my life

9. I can handle the abundance of the universe

10. Creativity flows through me with abundance

11. Abundance flows through me

12. I see every opportunity that comes my way

13. The world is good and there are no limits.

14. More good is waiting to reach me than I've ever experienced or imagined before.

15. All of my dreams are coming true

16. The universe provides for my every want and need

17. I attract talented hard working people

18. Life is fun, easy and over-flowing with abundance.

The words you speak into your own mind are powerful. They are even more powerful than the words you speak to others. Speak positive; speak victory, abundance, wealth, happiness, health and everything you are dreaming for.

Be reminded from this day forward when you speak, make a conscious and deliberate effort to have a minimum of ninety five percent of your daily conversations positive, purposeful, and profitable. This will strengthen your mindset, create possibilities and attract more abundance and wealth in your life. Every time you say or think something negative, stop! Immediately tell your mind *"cancel, clear"*. This one practice will dramatically transform your reality. Become unstoppable by using your words to create your next breakthrough.

You are in control! Take charge to turn things around in your life. In order to overcome the challenges you are facing, keep a positive mental attitude by reading or hearing something positive and staying away from *noxious* people or spend as little time as possible with them. If you are going through a difficult situation, or working on some new ideas or projects, give one hundred percent of your focus and make sure you stay on track, and get unstuck.

The wrong people will drain your power, creativity and bring out the worst in you. Give yourself the possibility of winning the game. Spend your time on building your dream! Grow yourself bigger, wiser and better every single day to become the higher level of a person who is capable of make it BIG despite the odds. By developing yourself you will become more peaceful, more positive, and able to think more clearly.

You are the solution. Power up your dream, decide to be relentless. Build your mind to accomplish your dreams before you see them by your eyes. Remember, all accomplishments take place twice; first in the mind, and then in reality. Claim what you want. Experience the emotion and the exhilaration of reaching your goal.

See it in your mind's eye as done. Put forth your best effort and see doors open. Opportunities and support that you cannot imagine are on their way now. Make it happen! Success and failures depends much on your *attitude*. Take full responsibility.

Law #2
Set Clear GOALS.

Setting goals is the first step in turning the invisible into the visible. Tony Robbins

---

A goal is a very important element to what you want in life. It is solely a clear picture of what you want to achieve in life. It determines what you're going to be, and actually a link between where you are and where you want to reach.

Goals are what we need for the future. We dream for the future, but live in the present. That is the way life has been designed, we look long-term and live short-term. Unfortunately, the present can create numerous burdensome obstacles. But setting goals provides long-term vision in our lives. We all need powerful, long-range goals to help us get past those short-term stumbling blocks. Fortunately, the more powerful our goals are, the more we'll be able to act on and guarantee that they will actually come to pass.

Think about this for a moment; "have you ever really sat down and thought through your life purpose?" if you haven't ever asked yourself such a question, better you do it. The reason why you should ask yourself if that; the answer to that will guide you to take the time to truly reflect and listen quietly to your heart, to see what dreams live within you. Your dreams are there, and they are the roadmap to your life purpose. Everyone has them. They may live right on the surface or they may be buried deep from years of others telling you they were foolish, but they are there.

Ask yourself this question "what do I desire in life"? In fact this isn't what you already have or what you have accomplished so far, rather it is what you really want out of life.

Once you have figured that out, POWER TO YOU! It's time for decisions to take a new route to success. *Take time to be quiet with no anything to distract you so that for a moment, you can truly take your mind away from the noisy, rushing and busy* world. Have times of quiet so that you can squint deep within for setting your hearts free to soar and take flight on the wings of your own dreams. Schedule some quiet "dream time". No other people, no cell phone, no computer. Just you, a pad, a pen and your thoughts. When you are quietly; *think of what really thrills you, get your heart beating and blood moving in every vessel!* Find the answer to the question "what would I love doing, either for fun or for a living? What would I love to accomplish? What would I try if I were guaranteed to succeed? What big thoughts move my heart into a state of excitement and joy? When you answer these questions you will feel great and you will be in the "dream zone." It is only when we get to this point that we experience what our dreams are.

Write down all of your dreams as you have them. Don't think of any as too outlandish or foolish. Remember, you're dreaming! Let the thoughts fly and take careful record.

Now, prioritize those dreams. Which are most important? Which are most feasible? Which would you love to do the most? Put them in the order in which you will actually try to attain them. Remember, we are always moving toward action, not just dreaming.

To achieve a goal you must set one, and if you set goals you must achieve. Ask yourself this question. Without setting a goal, what can you achieve? Absolutely, northing. Goal setting is also the same as sowing. If you sow, you will reap. Setting goals is asking the universe to give what you want. So your "want" must be clearly known so that it shall be given.   Different from unsuccessful people, successful people know exactly what they want and set proper goals. Very clear goals. You can't get anywhere unless you know where you want to go. Think of the kind of a person you want to be. Think of the amount of money you want in your bank account, the lifestyle you want, and anything you desire.

Goal setting is a powerful method of designing our future by not only focusing on the kind of lifestyle we desire or achieving anything in life but also giving us the ability to hone in on the exact actions we need to perform to achieve everything we desire in life. Goals are great because they cause us to stretch and grow in ways that we never have before. That means, we build ourselves to become better so that we are able to achieve our goals.

One of the amazing things we have been given as humans is the unquenchable desire to have dreams of a better life and the ability to establish and set goals to live out those dreams. We can look deep within our hearts and dream of a better situation for ourselves and our families. We can dream of better financial, emotional, spiritual or physical lives. We have also been given the ability to not only dream, but pursue those dreams and not just pursue them, but the cognitive ability to lay out a plan and strategies to achieve those dreams. Powerful!

Designing your future through goals settings must properly be done through evaluation and reflection of your current situation. That gives you an objective way to look at your accomplishments and your pursuit of the vision you have for life and shows you where you are so you can determine where you need to go. That is to say, it gives you a baseline to work from.

List whatever it takes to achieve what you want. This goes hand in hand with looking what you want to change or create, or what choice you want to make in order to have different results. Please understand that, what you want is what you get. Therefore; whatever you want, let it be BIG! Don't set for small things, they are not for you. Set for greatness in life. I know it's hard to set for greatness if you don't believe in your mind that you deserve and you can truly get. But let me tell you, if you set bigger goals that you don't believe you can accomplish and start planting them in your subconscious mind, it will start working for them twenty four hours a day. As the results you will start believing and working for them automatically without even thinking about! Like a magnet, you will start attracting bigger things in your life and end up achieving them. Sadly, most of us set small goals. In the other hand however, most of us don't shoot for the stars or moon and miss, but we shoot for the roof and hit.

Don't only set goals, but set meaningful or proper goals. Your future depends on how you set your goals. Ambiguous goals produce ambiguous results. Incomplete goals produce incomplete futures. There is power of accomplishing your dream in proper goals setting. It has been said; "a goal properly set is halfway reached". Learning to set a proper goal will make a very big difference in your life in a way you have never thought possible.

Many people have never achieved the lifestyle they want because of several reasons. Among these reasons, here are two. One, *they don't know exactly what they want*. If you don't know what you want the chances are good, *you'll end up some place else.* Two; they don't know how to set proper goals and discipline themselves to achieve them.

It doesn't matter how many times you have been struggling to reach your life goals, mastering this important skill will surprise you. Yes, you'll be surprised if you master it well. However, this skill is learnable; anyone can learn and master it.

Before looking on steps for proper goals setting, let me take you to the importance of having goals in your life. The following are your *why* in goals setting.

Goals Gives you laser Focus. Goals give you a single focal point to place all your attention in it at a time. When you don't have goals, you are aimlessly swinging around every day. Your valuable energy will be randomly dispersed in ad-hoc activities which you engage on whimsical basis. These are activities that play no role in your larger scope of life, but you are not aware of because you are just living life as it is. You end up mislabeling a lot of *'nice-to-do'* activities as important. You might also be engaging in these *nice-to-do* activities because you can't think of a better way to spend your time. You may have a broad idea of what you want to do. But until you clearly articulate it out as specific goals, you are not channeling your efforts properly. You will often find yourself getting sidetracked because you don't have goals to rein you in. It's really quite easy to get swept away by the currents of everyday life, simply because there are so many stimuli out there in our environment.

Goals setting save time and effort. The twenty-eighty rule says that the first twenty percent of time that you spend planning your goal and organizing your plan will be worth eighty percent of the time and effort required to achieve the goal. Planning is very important. When you have a Goal and a Plan, you increase the likelihood of achieving your goals by ten times. That equals to a thousand percent!

Goals allow you to measure progress. By setting goals for yourself you are able to measure your progress because you always have a benchmark to compare with. The smart way of goals setting involves setting deadline and sub-deadlines. These enable you to breakdown your goals into year to year activities, which can be subdivides into monthly activities. Monthly activities can be subdivided as well into weekly activities, which can be further subdivided into daily activities. That alone will help you figure out each day what you have accomplished by making an assessment on how you have performed in a particular day as you move to the endpoint. Without setting smart goals it'll be very hard to have this evaluation. As the results you can be in a movement to the direction of failure!

Goals keep you locked in and undistracted. By setting goals you give yourself mental boundaries. When you have a certain end point in mind you automatically stay away from certain distractions and stay focused towards the goal. If you have goals and visualize them to be planted to your subconscious mind, your will automatically start to be focusing only on your goals. Your subconscious mind will work on them twenty four hours a day and therefore it will direct you to all the activities necessary to accomplish your goals. For this case it is impossible for you to be distracted by something that doesn't take you to the direction of your goal's accomplishment.

Goals give you motivation. The roots of all the motivation or inspiration you have ever felt in your entire life are goals. Goal setting provides you the foundation for your drive. By making a goal you give yourself a concrete endpoint to aim for and get excited about. It gives you something to focus on and put one hundred percent of your effort into and this focus is what develops motivation. When you are going through tough times, it is sometimes easier to get discouraged. But if you have goals, you will find the courage when you look at their beauty and imagine the feeling of excitement you are going to have when you achieve them. That will always push you when you are down!

Goals make you accountable. Having goals makes you accountable. Rather than just talking about what you want all the time and not do anything concrete about them, you are now obligated to take action. Setting a specific goal gives you clarity on whether you are living up against what you committed yourself to do when you first set your goal. This accountability is accountability to yourself, not anyone else. This accountability is what you hold up to when you choose to read books or waste your time watching unhelpful TV programs. It is what you answer to when you spent that hour listening to tapes for self development rather than random web surfing. When you stay accountable toward your goals, you are staying true to your desires.

"Nobody ever wrote down a plan to be broke, fat, lazy, or stupid. Those things are what happen when you don't have a plan." ~ Larry Winget

We are goal designed creatures, which is the truth. Unfortunately this is affected by our habits. That's why we must discipline ourselves to changing all our habits which limits our true potentials for success. On the other hand, we must develop and maintain only those which empower our behaviors towards accomplishing our major goals in life.

Here are the proven goals setting techniques which works. They have transformed the lives of millions of people all over the world. They have been used by successful people for achieving their success, take advantage of them. If you condition your mind to follow these steps of goals setting and put them to practice, you can accomplish anything you desire in your life. They are going to skyrocket your life in all the dimensions.

1. **Decide exactly what you want in your life.** The key question to here is *"what?"*. This opens the door for *clarity* to what you really want. **Specify** exactly **what** you want to achieve. <u>Visualize what you want in every key area of your life, be the finance, health, family or net worth</u>. For example if your goal is to be having more money, don't just say I want more money. You have to specify the exactly amount of money. If you desire $10,000, or $100,000 or 1,000,000 or any amount that you want, specify. If it's a car, be specific to what kind of a car. The same to a home and anything you want.

   If you want to lose some pounds in your weight, be specific to how many pounds you want to lose. Your goal must be understood clearly to the extent that anyone can read and understand.

2. **Write it down.** The study is done in different universities has proved over the period of twenty to thirty year period, people

with written goals ended up earning and having a net worth ten times greater than people without goals. A Goal must be written, otherwise is just a wish or fantasy. Writing your goals down is pulling them out of the air where there are no substances at all and you write them down where you have something you can see and touch. In goals writing there is a very powerful connection between the mind and the hand. As you start writing your goals you will be astonished what comes out in a paper.

And when you write your goal down you engage in activity called psycho-motor neurons activities. You activate your visual, audio and kin static powers. Whenever you write you program strait to your unconscious mind. It starts to work twenty four hours a day. Writing your goals down on a paper is the same as writing them in your heart. They become a seed. Research shows that only three percent of adults have written goals worldwide. Three! not thirty, and the remaining; ninety seven percent works for the three percent!

3. **Set deadline.** Napoleon Hill said "a goal is a dream with a deadline". Every goal you set should have a timeframe attached to it. One of the powerful aspects of a great goal is that it has an end. That is a time in which you are targeting to its attainment. As time goes by, you work on it because you don't want to get behind, and you work diligently because you want to meet the deadline. You also have to break down a big goal into different parts of measurement and timeframes. For example; you can breakdown the five, ten or twenty years goal into year by year, so that you know how much you have to save and invest each year. From year by year you can then break them further into month by month, week by week and smart enough, break them into daily activities. The more you break your goal the more you are likely to achieve. If for some reason you don't achieve your goal by the deadline, simply set a new deadline. There are no unreasonable goals, only unreasonable deadlines.

Your subconscious mind uses deadlines as *forcing systems*. They drive you consciously and unconsciously towards achieving your goals on schedule.

4. **Make a list of everything you will have to do to achieve your goal.** In achieving any goal, you need a definite plan and act on that plan. The plan is your roadmap towards your goals. It is the answer to the question, "how I'm I going to reach my goals? This is something that requires true mental fortitude, and that's written out and planned in a diligent fashion.

5. **Visualize your goals.** Create clear, vivid, exciting, emotional pictures of your goals as if they were already a reality. See your goals as already been achieved. See yourself enjoying the accomplishment of the goal. If it's a car, imagine yourself driving this car. In fact go down and test- drive the car for you. Get a feeling for it, smell it. Take a picture of yourself driving that particular car and look at it in a regular basis. If it's a vacation, see yourself in the vacation already. Get the pictures in a brochure and put them in your house. If it's a beautiful home see yourself in a beautiful home. Walk to beautiful homes that are for sale. Start visualizing it, and getting the picture. Imagine yourself owning it. This will start attracting possibilities in your life for owning your home. A mental picture combined with an emotion has an enormous impact on your subconscious and your super conscious mind.

Law #3
Conquer FEAR.

Too many of us are not living our dreams because we are living our fears.
— Les Brown

At the University of Dar es salaam, there was a lady who had a very big fear when it comes to examinations! No matter how hard she prepared, her fear was so intense that she couldn't control herself.

In fact, what she feared was failing! She was an employee, highly paid by a company she worked. She was sponsored to pursue further studies as the way of being promoted to the highest rank job position. Therefore, however, she was afraid of losing the job and the highest position.

One day, she was doing one of her last exam in completing her course. Unfortunately, she found the exam so hard that she couldn't answer most of the questions. She thought for a couple of minutes what to do.... and came up with an idea. She decided to fake an illness. Shouted and collapsed down. The supervisors came and picked her up carrying outside the examination room where they called for an ambulance to take her to the hospital.

The diagnosis found her with fatal malaria, and immediately she was admitted for treatment.

Remember this lady wasn't sick, even any sign of sickness before! But the moment she reached at the hospital she was shivering with high fever.

What is the lesson?

Fear can be a source of a malady. Fear can be crippling. Fear can be debilitating. Fear feeds resistance and stops us from achieving dreams, from challenging the status quo, from using our voices, from trying something new and in fact leaving a legacy to the world community. The truth is that fear, is an emotional feeling that every human being has. We are programmed by our environment to have fear from our background. And this has been taking place through various ways. It is within us all ways out! No one is exempted. As we realize how it ruins our life, there is a need to overcome its consequences by turning it into a powerful tool or a milestone in living our dreams.

One of the best things to turn fear into elevator for your success is to decide what is it that you are going to stand for no matter how big the fear seems to be! Focus on finding your life purpose and be very clear for what you really want for yourself and your life, when you are clear on your why, you can then begin the journey to achieve. It is when we are not clear to what we want when fear takes over and start managing our life. Be clear to whatever you want in life and start acting in spite of fear. The more you keep on acting the more it gets out of your way, and soon you will turn it into faith. It is in this point where you now have begin the journey to achieve what you desire from your life and enjoy longevity in your success because you are living your dream, not fear.

In most cases we fear for the future. We question "what will happen?" sometimes we imagine what is going to happen. So, we fear for something we have no any experience with! Take this from me; if you let fear dominate your mind, it will find the False Evidences Appear Real! however, it is important to bring our over thinking mind continuously into the present, focusing on what needs to be done *right now*, and take action and get on with it. Action allows us to overcome fear and inertia because by taking action, by doing it anyway, by being brave and going for it, we feel back in control.

If your major fear is the fear of failure, don't let it blindside you. Get started and expect to fail! Go on failing. But here is what you want to know; with every failure, there comes a lesson that makes you really smart. Your life will be added values that will pave a new way to success. Failing will make you stronger, knowledgeable and wiser. To be successful you must once be a good failure. This is the secret of success that every successful person will tell you for they once failed and failed and even failed until they became successful.

I didn't understand this secret before when I was starting business. I was fascinated eye-opened by my mentor when he told me; *"go for failure"*. It was a difficult concept to me at that time. But with time when I was practicing it, I was able to realize changes in life. It wasn't easier to handle failures in my life, but I focused my mind on keeping on and learn from every failure until I succeed. When I opened door for failure, I noticed the more I failed, the smarter I became.

In going for my dream, I decided to quit my full time job. I really knew that, no one in my family is going to understand me on that. But I had to, because I was determined to make a difference in life. I started building my business in a full time basis. But guess what? I failed and ended up in bad debts. Things became worse when I had a family to take care, bills to pay, and yet, I was flat broke! I was ridiculed to the extent that I saw myself dumb stupid!

Several months later, my financial situation was so bad that my wife and I decided to go to my sister in-law. We had no money and business failed. I moved to another city, leaving my wife at her sister. To that new city I lived to my friend's one room house he had rent!. By that time I was seeking for a job. After sometime I got a job, rent one room and called my wife to start new life in another city.

As we were living, I still was restless! I still had a burning desire to build my business. at this time, my wife was not in my side. She reminded me of all the sufferings we had gone through when we were broke. But that didn't stop me. I still had a mission to accomplish in life. I decided to start business part time for a couple of months. But it wasn't growing since it needed to be paid big time. I decided to quit my job and build my business.

You want to know what happened? I was broke again! My wife decided to pack out with my 2 years old daughter. It was a very hard experience to separate with my loved wife and daughter. I was this time dealing with two challenges; first, the pain of losing my lovely wife and two, dealing with my financial difficulties.

Two months later, I was no longer able to pay rent and bills. This time I decided to go to my brother in another region which in the country side. I spent time reading books, meditating and gathering my emotional strength ready to start all over again. I used this time also to write my strategies for winning the game. After one month I moved back to start all over.

I was able to get a job in two days and started working full time and building business part time. This time things were going! I was able to start my company and the rest are becoming history.

Today I'm thankful for all the lessons I learnt from my failures. I'm better that anyone who has never failed. I have grown up to become a new level person who is not looking to fail in small things!. I'm now looking for the new level of challenges which are much bigger. It is when we are able to face bigger challenges when we are able to reach the higher level of success. the key lesson here is that; don't stop looking for challenges. That is equal to say, don't stop looking for bigger failures. There are better lessons to learn to succeed.

Let me tell you, successful people see fear as a curtain that blocks their vision to the room of plenty! They open or cut it to see how worthy their lives are. But unfortunately the same curtain appears as a jumble of rocks to unsuccessful people that limits them to make a difference in life. Two men can stand on one place, but they can never see and experience the same things. However, what you see and experience around you are the results of the choices you make.

We are living in the world of possibilities. We are living in the loving universe that opens up doors for greatness. Our task is to widen our vision and face our small inner voice that gives birth to fear, doubt and draw a line of impossibilities around us.

You hold yourself when you don't make decisions because of a fear of failure. You are closing the doors of learning to be successful in life. So be willing to challenge yourself being accountable for your own success, and ultimately your own happiness. Dig deep and share your unique talent, your thought leadership, your expertise or anything by creating energy. I promise you, that energy will drive change for you and those around you.

It is those who take the leap to face their fears who are able to create momentum towards their dreams. And it is that momentum which smashes obstacles along the way and keep them moving. No matter what it is, don't let your fear hold you back and stop you from living your dream. Learn to overcome it; it has nothing to do with you. Face it. Let it motivate you and ignite the fire within that will consume it in smoke!

You are powerful beyond measures. You can't let fear stop you like majority of people in the world who are not living their dreams because of it. By the way, there's nothing living called "fear" that can do you any harm. There is a Japanese proverb that says; Fear is only as deep as the mind allows. Therefore, fear is merely an imagination that takes place in your mind. it doesn't exist somewhere else!

Like negative thought, fear is destructive! Raise the rent and kick it out of your mind. It doesn't belong there. Don't accommodate it any more. Avoid it very hard, don't be afraid of it. It isn't there to scare you, rather to make you realize that something is worth it. Decide to become fearless.

Face the things you fear the most, be the fear of failure, fear of losing, fear of rejection, fear of poverty, fear of being separated from your loved ones, whatever it is! You are stronger than you give yourself credit for. Give yourself permission to confront your greatest fear, because on the other side a new life waits for you. Give yourself permission to grab procrastination by the collar, and say "*get out of my way*".

Make up your mind to live a life with no regrets. Decide to look all your excuses in the eye and make them stepping stones to your dreams. You owe it to yourself to take a chance on you. Give it your best, and find a way to reach beyond what you think is possible to make your mark.

Live on the edge. Playing safe is not an option. Place all bets on you. It is your time to win. Trust yourself, cast away fear, and kick doubt to the curb. Make the decision to call your own shots. Don't be afraid of what other people will think and say about you. What people think of you is none of your business. Listen to your heart, believe in yourself, and pursue your dream as if your life depends upon it, because in some cases, it does!

Don't allow your fears to run your life. See fear for what it is ~ False Evidence Appearing Real. Don't give up your power to the critics in your life. Trust yourself and believe in yourself and your dream. You don't need anyone's approval but yours!

Don't allow negative people or a stressful job to consume your life. Protect yourself. Develop the courage to do what you need to do. Your ability to be healthy, happy and prosperous matters! Make the decision to do what you need to do in order to have what you want to have. Give yourself permission to live life on your terms.

> *Rich people act in spite of fear. Poor people let fear stop them.*
> T. Harv Eker

Law #4
Get STARTED.

The secret of getting ahead is getting started. Mark Twain

Sometimes the hardest thing about success in life is just getting started. Getting started is the point where you have made a decision to begin doing something you desire. If you don't decide to start, still you have made a decision. <u>All the decisions; getting started or not to, have consequences. We have the opportunity to choose what we want in life, because I strongly believe that, life is all about the choices we make.</u>

In understanding this concept, please do yourself a favor. Just look the last ten years back and ask yourself, were there times when you could have made a decision that could have made your life ultimately different from today? It might have been a career decision, business, reading a book, listening to tapes, attending a seminar, starting exercising, start saving your money, changing your behavior, moving to another city or home, changing your career, starting a new job, changing friends, or anything. Take a moment and ask yourself, how these decisions have brought you to this point in your life? Is there anything you are thankful for or regretting for your decisions?

There is power in decisions to getting started. It is the point where everything happening in your life right now began with. Your decisions determine if you are going to make a difference in a positive or negative way. It is the only moment with a direct connection to your destination. The decisions you make at any opportune moment, will shape how you feel and set a direction of the person you are going to be tomorrow and in the entire future.

When I was looking for a mentor, my friend referred me to Stanley. I didn't know the guy before, but I heard from my friend that he is an entrepreneur who will be willing to help me if I ask for help. I didn't even bother myself asking more questions, I asked for his phone number and made a call. "Hallo Mr. Stanley, Habel is online. I was given your phone number by my friend Collins". "Collins?", "Yes, Collins" I answered. "I'm committed to start building my business, but I would like to have a mentor. My friend referred me to you. He told me that you are a nice guy who is ready to help me" I said. "Well Mr. Habel. Please let us meet next Wednesday, at 3:30 at the coffee shop" he replied. "It's okay Mr. Stanley, thank you very much. See you then".

On the day of appointment I arrived a half an hour before, keen to meet the guy. At exactly 3:30 pm he showed up.

What I realized from him is that, he is a strong man, kind, and understanding. I liked him in the first few seconds as he introduced himself to me and told what he is doing. Wow…! He is the right kind of a person I have been looking for. He is a successful entrepreneur, owning a successful airline company. I was willing to learn everything from him so that I can become successful too. As we were in our conversations for a couple of minutes, he asked me about my goals. I shared with him. Then he asked me a question, "what's holding you back from getting started?" "My big problem is financial capital", I replied.

He put his hand in his trouser's pocket and picked a key for his car and asked me, "If I give you this key for my Mercedes-Benz and tell you to come with only $ 1,000 so the car can be yours, will you be able to get the money?" "Of course, I can get", I replied quickly with excitement! "You don't have any excuse, get started going for your dream", he said. "…$ 1,000 is all you need to get started". That was a big lesson I have ever learnt. I was so much inspires with the guy. Moreover, I was thinking on how I could get started making my dream come to a reality. Several weeks later I started my business. I stopped procrastinating and thinking of a big amount of money to get started. I invested about $ 1,800 in my first business.

The truth of the matter is that; the hardest step in achieving anything is making a true commitment to get started and staying on track. Procrastination is the major reason that holds most of the people from living their dreams. They don't decide to get started by lingering longer in the questions and doubts that paralyze them from getting started.

The point to keep in mind is the fact that, getting started is the secret of success. Things cannot be done unless you get started. Don't wait. Take one step to the direction of your dream and I promise you, everything will be OK.

Don't labor forever over the question of how or if you can do it. Get started. Most of the successful people had no enough knowledge and skills of what they wanted to do, but that didn't stop them. They decided to get started immediately taking steps necessary for success, because they are clear on what they really want for their lives. On the other hand, they stay on track until they are successful. Unsuccessful people do the opposite, they are slow to get started and change their minds quickly, always bouncing back and forth. Get started but also be committed to what you have started to the point you find yourself accomplished your major goals in life.

Life is short, fragile and waits for no one! Don't wait for any reason. There will never be a perfect time to pursue your dreams and goals than NOW. Don't wait for things to get easier, simpler or better. Life will always be complicated. Decide now to start taking steps towards accomplishing your major goals in life. Otherwise, you'll run out of time. Excuse me, let me say it again. Don't deceive yourself waiting for things to get better, because they won't anyhow! Sure, they won't. Expect them to be worse! But if you start, you will find a way. My mentor has a principle "*don't wait*". He taught me to make decisions and get started immediately to build the things that will end up building me.

When you wait until tomorrow by thinking that you aren't ready today, tomorrow will come still you won't get started. Your mind will convince you that you have to wait until the next day. When the next day comes, again you will not be able to start. Your brain will be programmed to believe that; time is not right for you. This situation will continue until the time when your brain will tell you "it's too late to get started".

Everyone desires for success in life. But not everyone takes the first step to success. Ninety eight percent of people never make up their

54

mind about their major purpose in life. They never made decisions to get started to work towards their dreams. They just live in a beautiful world of wishes and fantasies. People who are always wishing are those who are entertaining northing than nightmares! Wishing is different from being committed. People who are committed neither wait nor look for excuses. They put their one hundred percent laser focus on their dreams.

You are different from "*wishers*". Even if you were among them, you now have learnt a valuable lesson that has pushed you from wishing to being committed. Therefore, I call upon you; give yourself permission to grab procrastination by the collar, and say "*get out of my way*". Make up your mind to live a life with no regrets. Decide to look all your excuses in the eye and make them stepping stones to your dreams. You owe it to yourself to take a chance on you. Give it your best, and find a way to reach beyond what you think is possible to make your mark.

Get started to work for your dream NOW. You can't accomplish it overnight, but your first step is what you need to get going to the finish line. It has been said; the journey of thousand miles begins with one step. You can't reach to the finish line if you haven't started. It's time for moving. There is nothing else to talk about, you have allowed fear to hold you captive long enough. You have thought…. "*I would…. but*". Push your "*but*" out of the way and get started. You have been procrastinating long enough.

You might be thinking… "*I'll start tomorrow*" I bet tomorrow will come and yet you will still say tomorrow! This situation will condition your mind to believe that time is not right. You will keep on lingering long enough and before you know it you will come to realize you are too late to get started. Get started my dear friend. Even you do not believe your own excuses anymore, get started. The writing is on the wall. You know in your heart tomorrow's results will never forgive you if you do not get started today. It does not matter what people say. They will say it and think it anyhow. But this is your life. Success and failure is on your hands. For that being the case, you have to take full responsibility.

Make your move before you are ready. Kick off all your fears, excuses and procrastination to the curb. Stop giving yourself reasons for standing still, failing to act, and playing it safe! Leap over your comfort zone, and decide to live a life beyond survival. Things may happen to you that you can not anticipate. Roll with the punches and keep moving. You have what it takes to get through any experience in life. Stay focused, determined and positive.

Tell yourself today no excuse is acceptable for waiting any longer. You deserve the best that life has to offer. The universe is on your side. Life is on your side waiting for you to take action. It will open doors that seem to be closed. Opportunities are going to present themselves in front of you. The right people will be attracted and all the resources needed for making your dream a reality.

I remember two years ago, I had a great business idea well planed and written. But I thought it wasn't the right time to start working for it. What was holding me back was "paralysis analysis" I thought I could start immediately when I get all the answers to my *"what if scenario"* however, I couldn't get some! A couple of months later, I heard people had started business with the same idea! As you read this book, the rest is history! Those people have made a fortune. The moral of the story is that; you don't have to wait. You have a great idea, start working for it. If you wait, someone will come up with the same idea and make a fortune leaving you the same year in year out. Successful people make decisions immediately, as long as all the facts are available. Unsuccessful people do the opposite.

It's time to go! Make your dream come true. Now is the best time ever. Don't wait, do something now that will take you one step ahead as you move towards your goals. Develop a sense of urgency in your own life. Stop putting yourself at the back of your own line.

Get up! Move forward and run towards a goal that will give you a greater sense of purpose, accomplishment, and satisfaction in your own life. Make it happen, or you will wonder *what happened!*

Start living the life that reflects your greatness, talents and fulfilled purpose. Kick off the entire excuses goodbye; they have nothing to do with your destination rather than holding you back. Never allow them to convince you to quit. Do yourself a favor, put them in a coffin and bury them before they buries your master plan and dreams.

Stop thinking, start acting. Thinking will never take you to your destination but action will do. Everything is on your hands! What you think you don't have is right here with you. As you start, you will see all the doors open. You will meet the right people, new opportunities and possibilities you never realized. *Be committed to design your future; don't wait for it to design you.*

Talk to yourself, pray and do whatever it takes to drag yourself in the direction of your dream. Your chance of winning may be slim to none. *Take slim!* You may be knocked down, but not knocked out. Come up swinging with everything in you. Life is on your side. The power to win is in your hands. Do not stop now, do not even think about it! Do not let a delay become a denial.

Change your strategy. The law of possibility is on your side. Go outside yourself. Ask for help and do not stop until you get it. Come back and look at it again with fresh eyes.

Focus on winning, not on the obstacles or challenges. Do not obsess and stress about what you need, or what is going wrong in your life. Keep working at it. You have to eat it, sleep it, breathe it and believe it. Open your mind to bold thinking and do not be afraid to take even bolder actions. Keep on reaching for your victory. Dig down deep. Release your inner strength and power.

What is not started will never get finished.
– Johann Wolfgang von Goeth

Law #5
Model SUCCESSFUL People.

If you want to succeed, model a successful person

Whenever you want to succeed, model a successful person. By modeling a successful person you will be learning successful habit and how to discipline yourself by doing what it takes for you to succeed. I persuade you to find a successful person you admire who is doing what you do or want to do and make your role model. However, the best way of learning is through mentorship. Look for a mentor. A mentor is someone who has gone down the road that you want to travel and can guide you to get to your destination faster than if you went at it alone. If you want to be healthy, you would find a mentor who is already healthy. If you want to be rich, then you have to find someone who is already rich. It has been said; *if you want to learn about money, learn from someone who has a lot of it.* Unfortunately most of the people do the opposite.

Successful people have wealth of knowledge which comes from the experiences of their life journey, moving from *pennies to fortune and from failure to success.* They offer their wisdom and experience so that we can be inspired to face our life challenges to live extraordinary life. They have a very big contribution in enhancing you life by resetting your sail based upon their experiences. You can easily see their trails that helps you to keep on moving instead of going through trial and error! You can take advantage to model them, learn from them and have their mentorship. They will hand you the gift of their insights so that you can change your plans, if need be, in order to avoid their errors. You can rearrange your life based on their wise advice.

Study successful people, find out what is it that they are doing and you are not doing. Learn how they behave towards money and success. Read their books, look videos and listen different audio programs on success. There are plenty of materials from successful people sharing their secrets for success. You can also attend seminars on success. This is twofold, one you will be able to learn on success and two, you are going to meet people of the same attitude. The experience is so powerful. And many of those people are successful already; it will be easier for you to learn from them.

If you don't model successful people the chances are good you are going to waste your time on *foolishness* or *foolish people*. Foolish people do not like to own responsibility for their decisions and never see the impact of their actions and choices on their lives. They will try to recruit you into their *madness*. They will attempt to convince you to pay their bills, pay their way and solve their problems. They do not listen to anyone, even though their life is in shambles.

Be focused to learning and growing to become a successful person. Don't settle for the mediocrity. You are destined for greatness. Let others be satisfied with being spectators, complainers and victims. You are a player on the field of life. You have dreams and goals that you are determined to achieve. You have drive and a desire to make your life matter. There are things that others find very enjoyable which just do not fit who you are. Be focused, relentless and hungry to make your life count. Be attached to only those of the like minded. You will be inspired, motivated and encouraged to reaching your goals.

Many of the successful people will wish for more people with the courage to ask. Don't hesitate to ask them. As long as you are applying this with respectful, many people are willing to help. The good side of this is that, people get to know who you are. And let them know that you take them seriously. It's a sign of self worth and also giving others the pleasure of helping you.

Surround yourself with (OQP) Only Quality People who are going to lift you to the higher heights.

I would like to share with you my experience with learning from successful people. We were travelling for business with my mentor Mike, a successful person who is self determined, hard worker and integrity. We were at the port, waiting for a boat. We sat for few minutes, and then he told me; "we have to go in the boat, one of my principles in life is; *don't wait*". As he was explaining it to me I was able to learn a valuable lesson that has transformed my life. I learnt that; successful people don't wait, as long as all the facts are there. But unsuccessful people do the opposite. They procrastinate. At the end they found themselves missing an opportunity or paralyzed with doubts and fear.

I also leant many valuable lessons from Ken Stewart, who had been my mentor for sometimes. He taught me to learn as hard as I could. "Learning will give you wisdom, and wisdom will make you successful". Previously I thought I don't have to learn because I thought I knew everything. But I came to understand that I was ignorant! I started learning every day, and that habit has not stopped. I will learn all the days of my life. Successful people learn, they invest a lot of money in learning. They never stop learning no matter how successful they are or become.

Your life will change from the books you read and people you learn from. It is also very true that your life will never improve until you look at an example or standard higher than you. Take your time learning from someone you consider your role model.

I'm giving you this example once again. When I was looking for a mentor, my friend referred me to Stanley. I didn't know the guy before, but I heard from my friend that he is an entrepreneur who will be willing to help me if I ask for help. I didn't even bother myself asking my friend more questions about the guy, I only asked for his phone number and made a call. "Hallow Mr. Stanley, Habel is online. I was given your phone number by my friend Collins". "Collins?", "Yes, Collins" I answered. "I'm committed to start building my business, but I would like to have a mentor. My friend referred me to you. He told me that you are a nice guy who is ready to help me" I said. "Well Mr. Habel. Please let us meet next Wednesday, at 3:30 at the coffee shop" he replied. "It's okay Mr. Stanley, thank you very much. See you then".

On the day of appointment I arrived a half an hour before, keen to meet the guy. At exactly 3:30pm he showed up.

What I realized from him is that, he is a strong man, kind, and understanding. I liked him in the first few seconds as he introduced himself to me and told what he is doing. Wow…! He is the right kind of a person I have been looking for. He is a successful entrepreneur, owning a successful airline company. I was willing to learn everything from him so that I can become successful too. As we were in our conversations for a couple of minutes, he asked me about my goals. I shared with him. Then he asked me a question, "what's holding you back from getting started?" "My big problem is financial capital", I replied.

He put his hand on his trouser's pocket and picks a key for his car and asked me, "If I give you this key for my Mercedes-Benz and tell you to come with only $ 1,000 so the car can be yours, will you be able to get the money?" "Of course, I can get", I replied quickly with excitement! "You don't have any excuse, get started going for your dream", he said. "…$ 1,000 is all you need to get started". That was a big lesson I have ever learnt. I was so much inspires with the guy. Moreover, I was thinking on how I could get started making my dream come to a reality. Several weeks later I started my business. I stopped procrastinating and thinking of a big amount of money to get started. I invested about $ 1,800 in my first business.

The key lesson here is; learn from successful people. They don't see obstacles, rather they see opportunities. They don't wait when an opportunity presents itself. They make decisions to get started immediately. They are also open in learning and being coached by other successful people.

Law #6
Find Your PASSION.

Stop chasing the money and start chasing the passion.
-Tony Hsieh

Most of the people are doing things they don't love. They are sick and tired of what they do! When they wake up early in the morning they think negative about their job, business or anything. This habit kills them emotionally, physically, mentally and spiritually. Unfortunately, they don't understand these are very crucial key areas that make any person complete. You won't grow and prosper if at all you are not developing yourself in these four important areas.

I think this is one of the reasons that makes most of the people die at the age 25 and get buried at the age 65! It isn't physical death that takes place first; it is emotional, spiritual and mental death then physical comes lastly. The key lesson here; do what you love and love what you do.

There is a friend of mine who invited me to join his business opportunity, I looked at it and thought I could make a fortune with it in a couple of months. I decided to get started. I worked very hard on it, but no any return. I went back to my friend; he taught me all the skills necessary to be successful. I went back and applied them, but they didn't work. I asked myself; "where am I wrong?" I couldn't find the answer. I was wondering. Working hard and applying all the knowledge, but nothing to show! I decided to invite my friend observe the way I do my business. "You are doing it right buddy", he said. "Why am I making so little?" It was very hard to find. My friend told me to be persistent. I did, but nothing changed.

One year later I decided to quit. At that time my friend was even more successful. The same business! What I came to understand is that; I was not passionate about it. I jumped to the business simply because I knew I'm going to be a multi millionaire, but I didn't like it. That was the root for my failure. Passion favors those who are going for it.

I also went through different jobs I was not passionate. I found my dreams were not coming true. I became negative to myself and started to fix the blames not the problem! I blamed my employer and other people thinking they were the cause of my troubles. So I was going from one job to another, one business to another but it seemed like failure was in my bloodline.

Five years later, I came to realize this secret. I decided to find out what I was passionate about. It took me a couple of weeks thinking of something I'm passionate. Finally, an idea came in my mind to start building my company. In the beginning it was very hard, but what I found is that; passion will make you survive in the storms of life.

Passion will make you survive the storms of life in anything you do, be a business, job or career. Remember success doesn't come easily. It comes with a lot of challenges, setbacks, failures and disappointments. If you have passion with what you do, you will survive when tough times knock you down.

Find something you love. Figure out what you are good at. There is a very big power in your passion. And that is your call in my opinion, answer it. It will unlock the secrets of your miracles.   You will find possibilities and great opportunities you have never imagined.

Success comes easier by doing what you love compared what you don't. Here is what you have to understand; when you do something you love, you allow your unconscious mind to work for it twenty four hours a day. This will control your performance automatically. On the other hand, it develops discipline. The truth of the matter is that, developing discipline is hard to most of us. It takes efforts and commitment and that's why many people are not successful.

Choose to live a stress-free life. Choose to follow your passion by dedicating all your efforts, knowledge, skills and experience to something you love. Choose to build your happiness and be thankful every morning when you wake up to start your day and say; *"I'm so thankful for this brand new day"* as you raise get prepared to work in accomplishing your major goals.

If your job doesn't make you happy and limits you from living to your full potential, find a way! I don't say you quit your job if you don't have to. Find an alternative. Find ways to tape your full potentials, build your happiness and increase your income. I know one of the reason why most of employees hate their jobs is because of <u>limited income</u>. However, the eleventh law in this book explains on different ways of multiplying your income.

We all know that successful people work hard. Isn't it? But here is what many people don't know; "successful people don't aim success in the first place, they do what they love and success comes automatically.

Dedicate your life doing what you really love and enjoy doing by giving it your very best. Life is too short to do what you can't give it your best. If you find yourself in that trap, please stop and get out of it. Don't linger long; you will get old before you know it! Every successful person you read about, they all say pretty much the same thing "*do what you love*". You'll do well and find the way to get it out of the world

Do what you love no matter what other people think and say; after all what others think about you is none of your business. Dance to your own music. March your own beat. It is your time to use all your knowledge, abilities and skills to bring out full expression of who you really are, what you love and what you want to accomplish out of life. You have what it takes to create a new life for yourself if you follow your passion.

Be unapologetic you when it comes to something you love. You'll be better at it more than the way you can begin to imagine. It sound much pretty simple, but I promise, you'll be surprised what will happen if you get this one right away.

Doing what you love acts like a magnet. It attracts the right people, resources, wealth and everything you want all the way to your destination. Nourish your physical, emotional, spiritual and mental strengths by doing what gives your life a purpose. Stay true to yourself and give yourself great satisfaction.

When it comes to what you love, be *insane*! Be the best at it by doing what others won't be able to do so that you'll have the things other people won't have. I like worlds of Martin Luther King Jr. *"If it falls your lot to be a street sweeper, go out and sweep streets like Michelangelo painted pictures. Sweep streets like Handel and Beethoven composed music. Sweep streets like Shakespeare wrote poetry. Sweep streets so well that all the hosts of heaven and earth will have to pause and say, here lived a great street sweeper who swept his job well.*

Law #7
Work SMART.

People who work hard and people who work smart have different measures of success. ~ Jacob Morgan

---

We have all heard the phrase *"work hard"* as the way of achieving success. It sounds right, but that is for the mediocre. If you want to go for greatness you should *"work smart"*. There is a very big difference between working hard and smart. Working hard is much more of physical abilities while smart involves mental abilities. Now, great achievers are the one who make the best use of their mental abilities than the physical abilities.

There is no problem with working hard, but here is the challenge; it doesn't cope with the changing world we have. It was the best way of achieving success the last centuries, right now it must be added another phrase for its activation... *"Work smart hard"*

Let me share with you the story of two hard working men, but one worked smart. It is a story by Burke Hedges about two ambitious young cousins who were best buddies and big dreamers named Pablo and Bruno. They lived side by side in a small Italian village.

They were both bright and hard working. One day an opportunity arrived when the village decided to hire two men to carry water from a nearby river to a cistern in the town square. Pablo and Bruno got the job, each man grabbed two buckets and headed to the river. By the end of the day, they had filled the town cistern to the brim.

Bruno, I have a plan, Pablo said the next morning as they grabbed their buckets and headed for the river. "Instead of lugging buckets back and forth for pennies a day, let's build a pipeline from the village to the river." Bruno stopped dead in his tracks ".
A pipeline!? Whoever heard of such a thing?" Bruno shouted. "We've got a great job, Pablo. I can carry 100 buckets a day. At a penny a bucket that's a dollar a day! I'm rich!

Pablo would work part of the day carrying buckets, and part of the day and weekends building his pipeline. He knew it would be hard work digging a ditch in the rocky soil.

The first few months Pablo didn't have much to show for his efforts. The work was hard, even harder than Bruno's because Pablo was working evenings and weekends too. But Pablo kept reminding himself that tomorrow's dreams are built on today's sacrifices. During his rest breaks, Pablo watched his old friend Bruno lug buckets. Bruno's shoulders were more stooped than ever. He was hunched in pain, his steps slowed by the daily grind. Bruno was angry and sullen, resenting the fact that he was doomed to carry buckets, day in, day out, for the rest of his life.

Finally Pablo's big day arrived, his pipeline was complete! The villagers crowded around as the water gushed from the pipeline into the village cistern! Now that the village had a steady supply of fresh water, people from around the countryside moved into the village and the village prospered. Once the pipeline was complete, Pablo didn't have to carry buckets anymore. The water flowed whether he worked or not. It flowed while he ate. It flowed while he slept. It flowed on weekends while he played. The more the water flowed into the village, the more money flowed into Pablo's pockets! Pablo the Pipeline Man became known as Pablo the Miracle Maker

Now, the difference between these two men is "smartness". Hard working gives the best fruits when integrated with working smart. Whatever you are doing, find a way to do it smartly. Because it is the only place where your fortune is hiding. If it is business, job or a career, focus to be the best by doing differently with more advances knowledge and skills that will make a big difference.

Always ask yourself; "how can I increase my performance?" then start writing down different ideas as they come to your mind to find the one that will be the game changer. Successful companies are working smart. I think that is the key point to focus on.

Your aim should not be the first or the biggest in anything you do. Your aim should be on being the best. Improve yourself every single day so that you will be in a good position. Improvement shouldn't be seasonal. You should never stop improving and finding smartest ways of performance.

Hard work doesn't allow you to fully use your brain, it pushes you for more physical work. It is better your incorporate it with smart work so that you will be able to use both your brain and the physical work if you have to.

Smart work is really important as it saves time and allows you to reach your goals faster than that of a hard work, it is the beginning of getting everything start working hard for you. Believe, you got it right. Everything will start working hard for you.

Working smart will help you create wealth by starting your business using (OPM) Other People's Money and (OPT) Other People's Time. One example of using OPM is to invest in real estate without putting your dollar! Many people have become millionaires by doing it, and yet more self made millionaires are emerging everyday in this business. The good news is, you can learn wealth creation using OPM and OPT and rise from zero to multi millionaire.

Working smart will enable you start passive income business that will help you access financial freedom. Financial freedom will allow you to live your decided lifestyle having you to work again if you don't have to! Working smart will break all the barriers to your business. It opens the gates of success when the business is going through challenges. It helps you find the right people to recruit in your business, the right resources, the right timing and the right ways of operating.

Working smart will help you systemize your business. Systemizing your business will take your business to the next level. It is the place which will give you what we call "Freedom". In this stage, you will be able to franchise it.

Working smart will help you create the so called multiple sources of passive income flowing to you every time. It is the best stage to enjoy the wealth that your business is going to reward you. It is the time when all your efforts and hard works are bearing ripe fruits. The list goes on and on….. The key point here is to *work smart harder*. Work on improving yourself and become smart. This will help you know where to direct your hard work.

We can learn from a story of a giant ship engine that failed. The ship's owners tried one expert after another, but none of them could figure but how to fix the engine.

Then they brought in an old man who had been fixing ships since he was a young. He carried a large bag of tools with him, and when he arrived, he immediately went to work. He inspected the engine very carefully, top to bottom.

Two of the ship's owners were there, watching this man, hoping he would know what to do. After looking things over, the old man reached into his bag and pulled out a small hammer. He gently tapped something. Instantly, the engine lurched into life. He carefully put his hammer away. The engine was fixed!

A week later, the owners received a bill from the old man for ten thousand dollars. "What?!" the owners exclaimed. "He hardly did anything!" So they wrote the old man a note saying, "Please send us an itemized bill."

The man sent a bill that read: Tapping with a hammer is $ 2.00, and $ 9,998.00 for knowing where to tap. Hard work is important, but knowing where to direct an effort makes all the difference.

Law #8
Invest in YOURSELF.

"In times of change, learners inherit the earth, while the learned find themselves beautifully equipped to deal with a world that no longer exists."
-Eric Hoffer.

Trust me on this. The best investment you can ever make is to invest in YOU, by acquiring the right knowledge, skills and information that will build you and make the best version of you. Learning will take you to the places beyond talents! Be a person with learning habit. Wherever you go, take with you some books. If you are in a car, listen to audio materials. Spend at least ten percent of your income to invest in learning. This is a successful person's habit. Learning never ends, it is a lifetime process. Make sure you learn as hard as you can if you want to make a difference in your life and the world.

Les Brown says, "If you want to be wealthy, you need to read at least thirty pages a day". We are bombarded with negative information every single day; the only way to get rid of them in our minds is to feed our minds with positive information that will replace them. Remember, if you don't do as hard as you can to build yourself up, chances are good you will be built with negative information, thoughts and ideas.

Be focused to learning and growing to become a successful person. Don't settle for the mediocrity. You are destined for greatness. Let others be satisfied with being spectators, complainers and victims. You are a player on the field of life. You have dreams and goals that you are determined to achieve. You have drive and a desire to make your life matter. There are things that others find very enjoyable which just do not fit who you are. Be focused, relentless and hungry to make your life count. Be attached to only those of the like minded. You will learn, become inspired, motivated and encouraged to reaching your goals.

Learning will not only change your attitude, but also reward you the kind of success you desire. Learning is the beginning of everything; be wealth, health and spirituality. Searching and learning reveals miracles in life. Through learning, the poor are enriched, ignorant educated, the lost find the way, seekers find and prisoners set free.

There are three basic ways through which you can learn. These are; *books, listening to audio CDs or MP3 recorded materials* and *attending seminars.*

Read books. By reading books, you will feed your mind with knowledge, skills and information that will help you in your journey to success. Successful people read a lot of books. Expand your mindset by reading something every day that stretches your imagination and strengthens your spirit. Gather the knowledge to create the next extraordinary version of you and to live your best life ever!

Here is the list of some books I recommend you read.

1. Think and Grow Rich by Napoleon Hill
2. The Secret by Rhonda Byrne
3. As a Man Thinketh by James Allen
4. Go getters by Peter B. Kyne
5. Rich Dad Poor Dad by Robert Kiyosaki
6. The secret of the millionaire mind by T. Harv Eker
7. *Magic of Thinking Big* by David Schwartz
8. The Magic of Believing by Claude Bristol
9. The Power of Positive Thinking by Norman Vincent Peale
10. See You at the Top by Zig Ziglar
11. Awaken the Giant Within by Anthony Robbins
12. How to Win Friends and Influence People by Dale Carnegie
13. Success Through a Positive Mental Attitude by Napoleon Hill and W. Clement Stone
14. Ask and Its Given by Esther and Jerry Hicks
15. The Laws of Success in sixteen lessons by Napoleon Hill

Listening to audio CD's or recorded MP3's. There are so many audio programs on how to create wealth. Personally I have listened to many audio books. I still listen to them over and over again. Every time I listen, I learn something new like I have never learnt before. I listen in the morning everyday when I wake up. And of cause this is the best time to listen or read at least few pages twenty minutes from the time you wake up. The reason why I recommend it; what happen is this time has the power to influence the entire day. So it is better you feed your mind with positive information. It will make you focused and effective the whole day.

Attending seminars. This is another powerful method of learning. This method if two fold; first it help you learn from successful people and experts who will show you how to succeed. Second, it connects you with like minded people. The experience is so powerful.

Broke people always think they know everything. They don't want to learn. However, that habit keeps them unsuccessful. It is until they become ready to learn when things will start changing. You can't get something new if you continue doing what you have always been doing. For things to change, the person you see when you look on the mirror must change. That is YOU. Yes, you have to change so that things will change.

Law #9
Never, Ever Give Up.

Never give up. Today is hard, tomorrow will be worse, but the day after tomorrow will be sunshine. ~ Jack Ma

---

Never, ever give up. The challenges you are facing are directing you to the right choice, which is… *"Changing your situation for the better"*. They give you a motivation that ignites the burning desire to become the kind of a person you want and live the lifestyle you have always desired. Keep reminding yourself; *"on these flames I'm standing, I have a choice to either let the situation change me or change it".*

I'm reminded of a story told. It is about a young woman who went to her mother and told her about her life and how things were so hard for her. She did not know how she was going to make it and wanted to give up. She was tired of fighting and struggling.

It seemed that, as one problem was solved, a new one arose. Her mother took her to the kitchen. She filled three pots with water and placed each on a high fire. Soon the pots came to a boil. In the first, she placed carrots, in the second she placed eggs, and in the last she placed ground coffee beans. She let them sit and boil, without saying a word. In about twenty minutes, she turned off the burners. She fished the carrots out and placed them in a bowl. She pulled the eggs out and placed them in a bowl. Then she ladled the coffee out and placed it in a bowl. Turning to her daughter, she asked, "Tell me, what do you see?" "Carrots, eggs, and coffee," the young woman replied.

The mother brought her closer and asked her to feel the carrots. She did and noted that they were soft. She then asked her to take an egg and break it. After pulling off the shell, she observed the hard-boiled egg. Finally, she asked her to sip the coffee. The daughter smiled as she tasted its rich aroma. The daughter then asked, "What does it mean, mother?"

Her mother explained that each of these objects had faced the same adversity - boiling water but each reacted differently. The carrot went in strong, hard and unrelenting. However, after being subjected to the boiling water, it softened and became weak. The egg had been fragile. Its thin outer shell had protected its liquid interior. But, after sitting through the boiling water, its inside became hardened! The ground coffee beans were unique, however. After they were in the boiling water, they had changed the water.

"Which are you?" the mother asked her daughter. "When adversity knocks on your door, how do you respond? Are you a carrot, an egg, or a coffee bean?" Think of this: Which am I? Am I the carrot that seems strong but, with pain and adversity, do I wilt and become soft and lose my strength? Am I the egg that starts with a malleable heart, but changes with the heat? Did I have a fluid spirit but, after a death, a breakup, or a financial hardship, does my shell look the same, but on the inside am I bitter and tough with a stiff spirit and a hardened heart? Or am I like the coffee bean? The bean actually changes the hot water, the very circumstance that brings the pain. When the water gets hot, it releases the fragrance and flavor.

If you are like the bean, when things are at their worst, you get better and change the situation around you. When the hours are the darkest and trials are their greatest, do you elevate to another level? How do you handle adversity? Are you a carrot, an egg, or a coffee bean?

There's something to learn from this story. We all face challenging times. But the difference is how we respond to them. We have choices, and each one leads to certain results. But the best choice is to change your situation to be better. If things get worse, don't be the worst. Be the best. This makes everything turn around in a way that brings meaning to your life.

Decide to become a *"no matter what"* person. Decide that you will make your dream become a reality, no matter what! Choose to be positive, choose to make your mind enjoy life no matter how it seems to be right now. Focus on the beauty of your dream. Focus on the opportunities and possibilities, not the problems.

It does not matter if you run out of money, or if life catches you on the blind side. It does not matter if you experience disappointments, failures or setbacks. You have what it takes to bounce back. Your gifts, talents and abilities require that kind of resolve. The next moment can change your life for good. Be open to that beautiful moment, it is tomorrow morning. Do not give up. You are able to make it.

I guarantee, successful people have failed many times than unsuccessful people. That's why they said wisely that, *"if you have never failed at anything, then you have never reached for a big enough goal"*. If you only choose goals that are safe, familiar and right, you will never stretch far enough to know who you really can become or what you are capable of doing.

To do something different, you will need to be someone different. Decide to leave your safety zone. Move beyond fear of failure to the possibility of authentically and consistently living your truth and creating a bigger life. Don't let failure hold you back, prepare to fail and fail until you find your way to success. Every time you fail, remind yourself; because you have failed does not make you a failure. Ask yourself, what did I learn? What was the lesson? Hold On, don't stop. You are more powerful than you think. Give up the excuses and keep moving forward.

There are circumstances in life you have to stand in a firm belief that; _if it is not one thing, then it's another_. At times when you are going through stinky stuff and everything around you seems turning the wrong way, and nothing is going your way, hold on. Don't stop! This is the right time to practice patience, faith and determination. The job you lost will be replaced by a career or business that you are passionate about. The person who is no longer a part of your life has made room for someone else who will truly love and respect you.

If it is not today, then it's tomorrow. If it's not this way, then it's the other one you are about to find. Perseverance, drive and moving forward with a positive mindset will help you to survive the storms of life. For now, your focus should only be on the bright side of life. It will rain on you again and you will be stronger for going through the storm. One day you will be thankful for the wisdom you gained and the person you became because of these tough experiences you are going through right now.

Be very careful with every negative thought coming to your mind. Do not let it take part a second! Discard it as soon as it comes. Protect your mouth from talking negative words. You are in the battlefield, load your weapon and go forward. Only take actions, never allow any negative or discouraging words. Be reminded of the fact that, death and life are in the tongue. Your words create your world and your world reflects your reality. You always have a choice. Use words that represent the highest and best expression of yourself and of what you see for your future and your life.

Live life on your terms. You have the ability to do that. Get still - regardless of what you are facing; be that finances, employment, or challenges with your family or relationships. Get still. This is no time to give in to stress, pressures that are put upon you, your fears or your circumstances. Look in the mirror and remind yourself that you are God's miracle child. Stand tall within yourself and resolve - where there's a will, there is a way. Say to yourself *"I am bigger than this"*

By now, you have had enough life experience to know your inner voice. It takes courage and conviction to trust yourself and follow your own mind. Cultivate the art of listening to you! Minimize the distractions, the noise, and the clutter in your head. Clear out the stuff, junk, and garbage. Practice listening to your own voice. It is the only way to live your life from a place of power.

I used to have a very tough experience in my life. It reached the time every muscle convinced me to give up. And I was about to! I called my mentor and explained to him everything I was going through. "Your dream is very important" he said, "the challenges you are going through right now are building you. You are becoming stronger, more focused and determined. Success is on your way. Don't stop pushing, you are about to see the light at the end of the tunnel". Those worlds gave birth to new hope in my heart. I started asking myself, *"if I give up, when I'm I going to live my dream"*? I was also reminded of the worlds which have been said *"most people die at age 25, but do not get buried until age 65"*. Do I *want to live a dead life?* From that moment I made a resolution with my heart. Committing that *"I will never exist with my real life on hold. I won't deprive the world of experiencing the real me!"*

Focus on things that build a stronger and more courageous you and that help you to get a good night's sleep. These may include mindfulness, chanting, meditation, deep breathing, laughter, prayer, enjoying silence and stillness. Read something inspiring, stretch and exercise your body and mind and practice gratitude. Life offers us abundant opportunities for laughter and tears. Put the good times in your pocket to savor. The challenging times go to your heart and soul. Your ability to handle life's challenges is a measure of your strength and character. Remember that no failure is permanent and defeat is not fatal.

You are in the middle of a miracle. Stand still and do not panic. Keep the faith. Continue to work your plan. Stay focused with a determined vision. Do not allow fear, failure, frustration, lack of money, discouragement, sickness, pain, or any temporary setback to kill your dream. You are bigger than any of these things. Take courage!

Believe that you can use any stumbling block as a stepping stone to a better life. Ask yourself *who can you count on? Who must you count out?* Reassess, regroup, and change your strategies. Come back with a vengeance! Resolve that failure is not an option. Keep looking up and moving forward. You can make it happen.

Keep looking for ways to win. Do not give up. You are closer to your next breakthrough than you think. Life is challenging you to be great. Do not back down. Dig in! Really stretch yourself. Talk to someone else for some new options. Make more phone calls. Get busy and keep it moving! Work harder for yourself and your dream than you would ever think of doing for anyone else. Make something great happen today.

Drink from the full cup of life. Taste the bitter, along with the sweet, knowing that all of it deepens your experience of life. Life is a rollercoaster. You will have ups and downs, unexpected drops, twists, turns and loops. Buckle your emotional and spiritual seat belt and hold on.

Choose to release your grip on the pain in your life, especially pain that is self-inflicted. Decide that you are not going to let the hurts you experience right now rob you of your future happiness. As you move through life, you will have experiences that can make you bitter or make you better. Remember you always have a choice. Choose to allow each experience to make you better and wiser. Grow through them. Continue to find ways to deepen and express the greatness within you.

Count your blessings. Gratitude is the fuel of resiliency. Train your mind to think of at least one thing for which you are thankful every day. It is often easy to overlook the small but significant blessings in your life. Look for positive things outside of yourself, because sometimes you cannot trust your mind. When you choose to look at the positives instead of focusing on the negatives, you strengthen your courage and your internal capacity to take on life. Look yourself in the eye and realize that you are ultimately responsible for working your way out of this situation. Give up the desire for things to be easy and deal with circumstances such as you find them. Know that you have the power to live a meaningful and happy life.

You have got only one life. One, I said. Yes ONE! Do what you have to do to get what you want to get, but don't give up. The easiest way to never give up is to remind yourself how resentful and regretful the rest of your life will become if you do. Let the words of Jack Ma remind you to persevere. *"Never give up. Today is hard, tomorrow will be worse, but the day after tomorrow will be sunshine"*. Guess what? Most of people who failed gave up tomorrow evening. This message is sending a picture to my brain; *"You'll never know that you were almost making it when you quit"*. Giving up is the ultimate form of self-mockery, self-humiliation and self-punishment. Trying again and again is the ultimate form of self-esteem, self-confidence and self-belief. Which one will you do?

Looking at the beauty of your dream and imagining how you'll feel when you achieve it the best way to pump yourself up when you're down. The choice you have is either to live your dream or leave it, alternatively. And if you chose to live it, go all in to pursue it. Because that is what life is all about. Don't let failure pin you down and push you against a wall. You have to fight back and look at every set back as a challenge that modifies you. You must always remind yourself however, being successful is all about having the courage, determination and perseverance to keep taking hits while moving forward.

You have something to contribute to the universe. You are the next success story the world is waiting to hear. Give it a chance to live and make the world a better place. The world needs dreamers like you. Remember how your dream is important by looking on how it could be if Steve Jobs had given up when he was fired from Apple? The world would never have seen the iPhones. What if J. K. Rowling had given up when she was rejected at Oxford? The world would never have seen Harry Potter. The world would never have seen John Lennon, Paul McCartney, George Harrison and Ringo Star if The Beatles had given up after being rejected by Decca Records. Look anything done that you see in this world; be reminded that, someone didn't give up.

Never give up on a dream just because it takes too long. Time will fly, but it will never come back again. Be encouraged, no matter how long the journey, everything is possible and promising as long as you have the courage to fight everything that's thrown at you along the way. You are potentially a winner. Yes you are! Winners aren't special people. They are just ordinary human beings who had the courage to put it all on the line for their dreams. Surround yourself with people who push you and encourage you to never give up, even if their words sound unrealistic. These are the people you will thank when you finally succeed.

Believe you are setting the foundation. It may look like you have no any result to show, but get to know that; you are growing the roots stronger. It will surprise you when things start to be seen. You will be glad and thankful for all the "hustles".

Your dreams may take time. That should not be something to discourage you. You have to know, the reason why your dreams takes time is that, they must lay a very strong foundation! It is exactly the same as the Chinese bamboo tree. You take a little seed, plant it, water it, and fertilize it for a whole year, and nothing happens. The second year you water it and fertilize it and nothing happens. The third year you water it and fertilize it, and nothing happens. The fourth year you continue to water and fertilize the seed but nothing happens! But during the fifth year, the Chinese bamboo tree sprouts and grows ninety feet in six weeks! Yes, ninety feet.

Keep on the faith, your bamboo tree is about to come out of the soil. Don't count how many times you have fallen! There is a proverb that says; Fall seven times and stand up eight. Falling down doesn't mean you are defeated. Defeat is when you are thrown down by your opponent in the ring because you got knocked out. Giving up is when you don't have the courage to get back on your feet and last another round. Never, ever, confuse defeat with giving up

There are no excuses for giving up. You might be able to convince someone else, but what will you say to yourself when you look in the mirror decades down the line and think about all the missed opportunities in life? Never give up. Great things happen to people who have the courage to go against the tide and win, no matter how long it takes.

I compare life to running a race. If your mind decides that you need to give up because you are tired, your feet won't budge. But if your mind decides that you must cross the finish line at any cost, your feet will run even when you are tired. Give up on your weaknesses, not your strengths. Give up on your enemies, not your friends. Give up on your nightmares, not on your dreams. You deserve the best life has to offer if you keep on keeping on.

I like the poem "Don't quit" by unknown author, take a look on it here;

> *When things go wrong, as they sometimes will,*
> *When the road you're trudging seems all uphill,*
> *When funds are low and the debts are high,*

And you want to smile but you have to sigh,
When care is pressing you down a bit,
Rest if you must, but don't you quit.

Life is queer with its twists and turns,
As every one of us sometimes learns,
And many a failure turns about,
When he might have won if he'd stuck it out.
Don't give up, though the pace seems slow -
You may succeed with another blow.

Often the goal is nearer than
It seems to a faint and faltering man;
Often the struggler has given up
When he might have captured the victor's cup,
And he learned too late, when the night slipped down,
How close he was to the golden crown.

Success is failure turned inside out -
The silver tint of the clouds of doubt,
And you never can tell how close you are -
It may be near when it seems afar;
So stick to the fight when you're hardest hit -
It's when things seem worst that you mustn't quit.

Learn to choose whether to hold on or give up from this story of two frogs. One frog was fat and the other skinny. One day, while searching for food, they inadvertently jumped into a vat of milk. They couldn't get out, as the sides were too slippery, so they were just swimming around.

The fat frog said to the skinny frog, "Brother Frog, there's no use paddling any longer. We're just going to drown, so we might as well give up." The skinny frog replied, "Hold on brother, keep paddling. Somebody will get us out." And they continued paddling for hours.

After a while, the fat frog said, "Brother Frog, there's no use. I'm becoming very tired now. I'm just going to stop paddling and drown. It's Sunday and nobody's working. We're doomed. There's no possible way out of here." But the skinny frog said, "Keep trying. Keep paddling. Something will happen, keep paddling." Another couple of hours passed.

The fat frog said, "I can't go on any longer. There's no sense in doing it because we're going to drown anyway. What's the use?" And the fat frog stopped. He gave up. And he drowned in the milk. But the skinny frog kept on paddling.

Ten minutes later, the skinny frog felt something solid beneath his feet. He had churned the milk into butter and he hopped out of the vat.

DON'T GIVE UP, OKAY?

Law #10
Be Disciplined.

Discipline is the bridge between goals and accomplishment.
~Jim Rohn

There is a direct relationship between discipline and success in every dimension of life. The number one reason why people don't succeed is because they can't discipline themselves to do the planning and preparation, and then the hard work necessary.

Discipline is one of the most important ingredients for success. Jim Rohn called it a *bridge* between goals and accomplishment. Pablo compared it to vitamins to the body by saying "always remember to take your vitamins. Vitamin A for Action, Vitamin B for Belief, Vitamin C for Confidence, Vitamin **D for Discipline** and Vitamin E for Enthusiasm.

Success is built on the foundation of discipline. Ask any successful person will tell you how important it is. Without it, I guarantee, you will never be successful. And if by chance you succeed in your job, career, business or anything…. sooner or later, you will find yourself in "good troubles"

I strongly believe, you will get everything you want if you develop the required discipline. It is important in a way that it helps you operate by principle rather than desire. It'll always be a reminder to impulses which are likely to take you out of the track and put you in full control of your performance. It deposes our futile attempt by redirecting our minds to the right path.

Human beings are solely creatures of habit. For this reason, you must shape your own personality to adopt successful habit. This can be done through repetition. Any act yielded to several times becomes a habit, and the mind is shaped to join the forces developed out of your daily habits.

Developing discipline is non-negotiable commitment for enhancing your life. Develop the required discipline for reaching your goals and be ready to pay the price. In the beginning it will appear as an overwhelming task, but if you are consistent, it becomes your second nature. Your subconscious mind will start working for it twenty four hours a day and you will start following without even thinking about it! Like magnet, it will pull you.

Build and maintain the discipline. Always look for areas of your life that needs to be changed; be it your relationship, finances, health, your work or life situation. Ask yourself - *"Who do I need to become and what must I do to make a major impact on this part of my life?"*. Give this area your undivided attention for a minimum of fifteen minutes each day for at least thirty days. Make this commitment non-negotiable.

Get out of your own way. You have something to do! Embrace discipline and self-control as a bridge to your new future. Make the decision to create a bold agenda for yourself and for those you care about. Hold yourself accountable for daily results that can be monitored and measured.

Therefore; discipline must be developed in several areas I'm going to explain them here below for you.

An attitude of gratitude.

I know it sounds like cliché, but it really works. An attitude of gratitude is the exactly opposite of a poverty consciousness. When you start to regularly think of the good things that you have, of how fortunate you are, that sends a strong message of abundance to your unconscious mind and creates a flow of prosperity. One of the single most important things you can do is make a practice every night before you get to sleep, thinking of all the good things in your life. Your job, health, friends, opportunities or business, and say thank you to God for universe, the life, whatever it is, that you feel comfortable to. *"Today's gratitude buys you tomorrow's happiness"*

Develop an attitude of gratitude by being thankful for everything coming your way, no matter how small it is. Build a strong faith of accomplishing something greater and better in your life that will change your current situation by taking you to the new heights of abundance, prosperity, health, freedom and wealth.

As you keep your mind and heart on track, start and end your day with gratitude, your will be empowered to live life to the fullest and enjoy the abundance life has to offer. <u>An attitude of gratitude opens doors of fullness of life. It turns whatever small we have into more than enough! It will take you from struggle and surviving into thriving, from the bottom to the top and from no one to someone. Be grateful, embrace this valuable behavior for turning things that worked against you start working for you.</u>

Be thankful for what you have; you'll end up having more. If you concentrate on what you don't have, you will never, ever have enough."
-- Oprah Winfrey

Manage your priorities.

How do you discipline yourself to be focused? Make a list of everything you have to do during the day, you set priorities on your list and then you start on your most important task first thing and you discipline yourself to keep working. Once you have decided on your most important task, resolve to concentrate single-minded on that one task until it is one hundred percent complete. Once you have developed the habit of completing your task, you will earn two and three and even five times as much as other people.

In goals setting you learnt on setting sub deadlines. That is very important in managing priorities and saving time. It gives you the chance to breakdown your long-term goals into month by month, week by week and even daily activities. Day to day activities gives you the daily 'to-do' list to be implemented. Make sure you write your to-do list of the next day before going to bed, your weekly activities a week before, monthly activities one month before and the activities for a year before starting the year. This is a powerful method of developing the discipline necessary for accomplishing your goals.

Always spend the time of your life on things that really matter. Stay focused; be committed to your list of priorities every single day. This is the best way of accomplishing the tasks you have planed within a timeframe. You will stop wasting time on unimportant things. You will always figure out what is most important to you and prioritize your life accordingly. Establish your priorities, start with most important things first and be committed until you accomplish them. Make this your habit and you will be able to see how good things happen when you get your priorities straight.

To succeed today, you have to set priorities, decide what you stand for.
~ Lee Iacocca

Have discipline with how you spend.

Come up with a plan to cut off unnecessary expenditures and clearing debts week by week or month by month. Develop a habit of writing down everything you spend, and then start looking for unnecessary expenses. Cut them off from your budget. Look for the ways to cut your expenditures so that you can start managing your money well. Remember spending is a habit, develop a good habit of spending. Live below your means. Rich people are living below their means!

Study wealth people. Find out what it is that they are doing that you want to build. Understand how they think and behave towards money and wealth. Do the technique they did or have a mentor to guide you in this area so that you can manage your money well. Find what rich people do and you haven't done it yet. Read the books and listen to audio programs on wealth. There's a program with plenty of superb sources of wisdom about wealth on the book shelves.

Law #11
Increase your INCOME.

Rule number one; never lose money. Rule number two; never forget rule number one.
~Warren Buffett

If you want to create or increase your wealth, you must increase your income. Rich people have multiple sources of income flowing to them in a continuous basis. The best way to do this is through reducing your expenses and increasing income.

Before looking on various ways to increase your income, it's better you know how to manage your money. Without managing your money well, you are NOT going to create wealth and access financial independence, no matter how big your income is. It's also important to know that the world gives what you can handle. T. Harv Eker put it clear in one his wealth principles. He said, *"Until you show you can handle what you've got, you won't get any more!" You must acquire the habits and skills of managing a small amount of money before you can have a large amount. Remember, we are creatures of habit, and therefore the habit of managing your money is more important than the amount*

This is very important discipline in creating wealth. It always doesn't matter how much you make, but what matters is how much you save. Many people earn a lot of money and spend them all. This is very dangerous for your financial future. Do as hard as you can to save at least ten to twenty percent of your income for your financial independence.

Make sure you save first before spending. Then spend only what you can truly afford. It sound obvious, but you have to condition yourself to do it well. Poor people don't follow this principle that's why they end up where they are because of the choice they make. They spend up to the last penny they earn, without saving a dime and yet, they start blaming other people and complaining their financial situation without knowing that the problem is not the money, it is them!

How do I Manage My Money?

"If you don't know how to care for money, money will stay away from you."
—Robert Kiyosaki

This is very important key lesson never taught in schools. It is taught in homes. Unfortunately most of the people are not taught this important lesson in their families. This is the reason why the rich get richer because of this kind of education learned at their home, in my opinion.

However, you can learn this important skill and become financially free. The only place you can learn is through books, seminars, video and audio programs, and from successful people.

Here are ways to manage your money and create wealth.

A. Savings

You aren't going to succeed in life without saving money. Yes, you heard me right. There is no exception to this rule, and no one may escape it. It is the way of acquiring riches, since big things comes in small portions, as you save and save you'll end up having "good money"

The best things you have to know are; why you should save, How to save and where to save.

Why you should save:

Saving is really important for your financial freedom. Financial freedom simply means living the lifestyle you want without having you to work or depend on someone financially. Savings also provide the ability to have funds to allocate to investment and a prosperous future, emergencies and funding expenditures or luxuries.

How to save

I think you have heard *"save any money left over, that you don't need for essentials or once you've paid your bills"*, right? BIG MISTAKE! You have to save first, and then spend what you can truly afford. Unfortunately people mostly do the opposite. They spend first then save what is left over, more often they even spend more than what they earn! And end up forming poverty.

Remember; saving is paying for your future. Make sure you have to develop this behavior of paying yourself first before any bill or spending. Save at least ten to twenty percent of every amount you earn.

Don't be intimidated by the behavior of spending; be committed to save money for your future. Since saving is a habit, if you haven't developed it, it'll be hard to master. What requires is to develop it. Start storing new files in your subconscious mind on saving. Make it a burning desire by setting a goal and writing it down. By doing so, you will be reprogramming your mind to accept this saving money habit.

Saving doesn't mean limiting your earning, it does the opposite. There is a myth to some people who believe the key of getting more money is spending more! Let me tell you; "the more money you save for your future, the more money magnet you become. The more money you spend without saving, the more money slave you become". So when you get money, the first thing to think should be saving, let spending come lastly.

Therefore, you should develop and follow systematic the behavior of saving at least ten to twenty percent of all the money you earn or receive for achieving financial freedom. It is very important. Without doing this, there is no any miracle you can become financially independent. The behavior of saving also develops other qualities for success.

Where to save

Dave Ramsey, the financial author noted, *"saving only $100 per month from age 25 to age 65 at 12% growth gives you $ 1,176,000. Everyone should retire a millionaire"*. Instead of saving your money with no growth rate, the best and simple way to start saving for the future, is to open a bank account with at least ten percent interest earned. You will be saving while your money growing. This is important in helping you to reach your financial goals quicker. There are some of the accounts with interest paid on a tiered basis, meaning that the interest rate increases as your balance increases – so the more you save, the more you earn!

B. Get out of Debts

Napoleon Hill puts it clear, *"unless you free yourself from debts you will forever be its prisoner. Debt amplifies the fear of poverty and greatly decreases your ambition and self-confidence"*

You should avoid debts, they are merciless master and a fatal enemy of the saving habit. Make sure you come up with a plan, and take steps towards reducing your debts week by week, month by month until you are able to clear all the outstanding debts.

C. Live below your means and cut your expenses.

Rich people live below their means. They are very careful in spending. Write everything you spend, then start checking where you should cut off and or reducing the expenses so that you begin paying all your debts and saving as much as you could for your financial freedom.

Actions

- o Start saving today at least ten percent of your earnings
- o Manage your spending and gradually increase your savings until you are able to save at least twenty percent of your income
- o Live below your means
- o Cut your expenses.
- o Save your money in an account with compounding of at least ten percent growth.
- o Get out of debts.
- o Invest your money wisely. You can choose to invest in passive income business, real estates, stocks or bonds.

D. Increase Your Income

Here are my suggestions for five basic ways you can increase your income and become financially free.

1. *Investing in real estates.* The best thing about this kind of business is that, you can do it part time. It also gives you an opportunity of using other people's money and corporate money to invest in the business. It doesn't need any capital from your pocket to get started if you do it smartly! You need the required skills on how to run the game. There are couple of courses on how to invest

in real estates. Take time to learn so that you can become successful.

2. *Using e-bay.* This is another way of increasing your income. You can get started to sell things on e-bay without any cash or capital and make a fortune. There are couples of good courses to teach you on how to sell in e-bay. Take advantage of this method to increase your income.

3. *Investing in the stock market.* You have the opportunity to invest in equities and stocks. It is a powerful way of creating wealth used by most successful people.

4. *Trading in stocks.* This is different from investing in stocks. Investing in stocks involves buying commodities, stocks or something this morning and sell this afternoon. Or buy today and sell in two or three days. You can do it part-time, and there are great courses on how you can trade in stocks. You can take advantage if this way of creating wealth ever since it doesn't require big amount of money to get started.

5. *Multi-level marketing/ network marketing.* Network marketing is the best business model that gives you the opportunity to build great wealth by starting with very low financial capital, with very low risk. It is flexible, you can build it part time or full time. I think this is the only business model which has provided opportunity for many millionaires in the world today. Ordinary people are earning extraordinary income. It is promising business if you are teachable, coachable and dedicated.

You are now ready for the 12th law, which will take you the next step up the ladder of Success that will not only bring you joy and the sense of satisfaction by living your life purpose, but also make you impact the lives of others positively.

Law #12
Leave a LEGACY

We should be ashamed to die until we've made a major contribution to humankind.
~ Horace Mann

I remember it was September 2014, when I had a chance to meet Mark Stevens one of the rich guys in America on one of his meeting to my country as he was launching his global company. He said worlds that really touched my heart and added more purpose to my life. He said; *"When you come to the end of your life, when you are taking your last breath. It isn't going to matter how big your house was, your car or all the material things you have accumulated for yourself, the only thing that matters are the lives that you have touched. And that will be your legacy"*

Use well the gift of life by being a blessing to others. Choose to give and make the world a better place to live. You are chosen to hold other hands and show them new hope in a way they never thought possible. Make them be thankful for your life.

You must live your legacy not only to your family, but also nation and the world community. That is what you have been created for.

Life is all about giving and serving others. It's all about giving your contribution to the world. This gives your life a fulfilled purpose that you have made some differences and in fact it shows that you have lived well.

We are all here on this planet to help others. It's the *love* that we have to give to the world. Think of people who have gone, but still we remember their contributions. Think about you, is there something you have done for others, which will leave your mark? If you are successful, and yet your success hasn't impacted other people positively, you are poor in your heart. And by the way, don't consider your life as a success. Here is what I know about successful people; they look for opportunities to help others. And if you are going for success, the vehicle is open. Look for opportunities to help others. Zig Ziglar put it clear this way; *"You can get everything in life you want if you help enough other people get what they want".*

When you are committed to help others, you will always find new meaning to your life. Give freely the gifts of love and compassion, without concerning yourself what you receive in return. But what you have to know is that; your life will become much better by making others better.

The days we are given on earth are numbered. You have to think how privileged you are for the gift of life by preparing yourself for your last day. Think of the legacy you leave on earth, not your wealth. But the quality of your life and how many people are grateful because of your life. Understand and know that life is not just about what you do. It is about how you serve and what you give! Go within yourself to grow outside yourself. Release your talents, use your abilities, and live with a spirit of adventure and boldness. Create a life where you make a difference, and leave your mark.

Leaving your legacy will give you the real wealth. Real wealth is feeling happy and having a sense that you are contributing something to the world, and feeling that your life is worthwhile.

The purpose of our lives is to add value to the people of this generation and those that follow. ~T. Harv Eker

PART THREE

Your Decisions, your reality.

The tragedy of life is what dies inside a man while he lives.
~Dr. Albert Schweitzer

I hope you have learnt a lot of things in this book, but more important, I hope you are ready to get started applying the laws for success to enhance your life. My wish for you is that; you have made the best decisions that, "time is now". It's my wakeup call to you; be unstoppable and ready to change your life now!

You have to start the going that will create a momentum of making a difference. The truth of the matter is; if you don't start, chances are good you are not going to accomplish your dream. It doesn't matter how beautiful or big your dream is, if you don't take steps, you are doomed!

In Part one of this book, I introduced the meaning of success, which is; living your life in a way that pleases you or getting whatever you desire and becoming the kind of a person you always wanted to be. This generalizes the definition of success, since every person has different perspective about being prosperous in life and is defining success in another way. Some might define success as having millions of dollars, luxurious cars and a huge mansion, whereas others consider a life full of joy and happiness with their family as the true meaning of success. So what you want to accomplish in life matters, and achieving, that is what you consider *success*.

In Part two of this book, you learned the twelve laws for success. I recommend you reread these laws over and over again so that you will be able to root them in your subconscious mind. Once you root these laws to your subconscious mind, they will pull you like gravity without even thinking! Your attitude will change and so do your life.

Be truly dedicated for what you are going to stand for, once you have figured it out. Start creating your testament to the world, that will make a difference by influencing the lives of others around you. It is when you have a sense of clarity and purpose for yourself and your life, when you can then begin the journey to achieve what you desire from your life, and really enjoy longevity in your success because you are living your life on fulfilled purpose.

Be determined to follow the inner voice that speaks victory in your life. That is the only voice that directs you to your destination. Don't be intimidated by the other voice that convinces you to doubt your ability. Don't pay attention to it. When it starts giving you all the excuses that you can't reach your destination, stand up bold to yourself and command it to shut up! Give yourself all the reasons why you can be successful. Visualize your dreams everyday and remind yourself of the excitement of accomplishing them. See yourself on top! See yourself living your dream and making a difference in life.

We all live in the same planet earth, we all breath the same oxygen and exhale carbon dioxide. We all have weaknesses and some liabilities. But why others become successful while others don't? why others see opportunities at the same place where others see obstacles? Why others thrive while others survive and struggle to pay bills? Why? Why....? Though we live in the same world, but we don't see and experience the same. That is to say, two men can stand in the same place, but see and experience different things. However, what you see and experience around you are the results of the choices you make. We are living in the world of possibilities. We are living in the loving universe that opens up doors for greatness. Our task is to widen our vision and follow our inner voice that speaks who we really are. The voice that speaks the fullness of our destiny and encourage us to stretch and keep on grinding.

You hold yourself when you don't make decisions because of a fear of failure. You are closing the doors of learning to be successful in life. So be willing to challenge yourself being accountable for your own success, and ultimately your own happiness. Dig deep and share your unique talent, your thought leadership, your expertise or anything by creating energy. I promise you, that energy will drive change for you and those around you.

It is those who take the leap, who face their fears who are able to create momentum in their success dreams. And it is that momentum which smashes obstacles along the way and keep them moving. No matter what it is, don't let your fear to hold you back and stop you from living your dream. Learn to overcome it; it has nothing to do with you. Face it. Let it motivate you and ignite the fire within you that will consume it in smoke!

You are powerful beyond measures. You can't let fear to stop you like majority of people in the world, who are not living their dreams because of it. By the way, there's nothing living called "fear" that can do you any harm. There is a Japanese proverb that says; Fear is only as deep as the mind allows. Therefore, fear is an imagination that takes place in your mind.

Take the hard way to success and get ready to pay the price by doing whatever it takes to live your dream. Develop the discipline necessary for your success by adopting successful behaviors. Successful behavior can be build by always practicing them. Remember, the person you become in the process of going for success is most important than success itself. We are able to see examples of successful people who lost everything in their lives, but were able to get back in a short period of time. The truth is that, they lost everything, but they didn't lose their successful behavior. That is what you need for your success.

Your dream is important to the universe, give it a chance become a reality. The world has been waiting for it for so long. Do not care how many times life has pushed you aside. You can make it. It doesn't matter what have been thrown at you, you are still valuable!

YOU ARE VALUABLE. Yes you are! Though it's hard to believe when you are down, but you have to believe it, anyhow. There is a story of a well known speaker started off his seminar by holding up a $20 bill. In the room of 200, he asked, "Who would like this $20 bill?" Hands started going up.

He said, "I am going to give this $20 to one of you but first, let me do this." He proceeded to crumple the dollar bill up. He then asked, "Who still wants it?" Still the hands were up in the air.

"Well," he replied, "What if I do this?" And he dropped it on the ground and started to grind it into the floor with his shoe. He picked it up, now all crumpled and dirty. "Now who still wants it?" Still the hands went into the air.

"My friends, you have all learned a very valuable lesson. No matter what I did to the money, you still wanted it because it did not decrease in value. It was still worth $20.

Many times in our lives, we are dropped, crumpled, and ground into the dirt by the decisions we make and the circumstances that come our way. We feel as though we are worthless. But no matter what has happened or what will happen, you will never lose your value. You are special - Don't ever forget it!

Believe, it is well with your future. Thank you so very much for spending your precious time reading this book. My wish for you is that your life be filled much with greatness. YOU ARE SPECIAL TO THE WORLD. Feel it when you are broken for it is easier to remember who you really are and raise to the top.

For your success,

Habel .H. Samida.

PART FOUR

ABOUT THE AUTHOR

HABEL .H. SAMIDA is a motivational speaker and author. He has taught and touched the lives of numerous people. Now for the first time, he shares his proven twelve laws for success in this book with astonishing results in changing your life for the better. Read it for your success.

He is so dedicated to change the lives of millions of people worldwide by sharing his story and principles for success. He wants you to make a difference in your life, family, nation and the world community by touching the lives of others and leave your legacy.

Don't miss the next revolutionary personal development and self-improvement book "**Sow the Seed of Greatness Within**" by your favorite author, which is going to be published in a couple of months.